EDUCATIONAL POTENTIALITIES

COLLECTED TALKS ON REVOLUTIONARY EDUCATION, AESTHETICS, AND ORGANIZATION

EDUCATIONAL POTENTIALITIES

COLLECTED TALKS ON REVOLUTIONARY EDUCATION, AESTHETICS, AND ORGANIZATION

Tyson E. Lewis

Foreword by Derek R. Ford
Afterword by Noni Brynjolson

Published by *Iskra Books* 2023

ISKRA BOOKS
Madison, Wisconsin
U.S. | U.K. | Canada | Australia | India
Iskra Books is an independent scholarly publisher—publishing
original works of revolutionary theory, history, education, and art, as
well as edited collections, new translations, and critical republications
of older works.

ISBN-13: 978-1-0881-1690-6

British Library Cataloguing in Publication Data
A catalogue record for this book is available from the British Library

Library of Congress Cataloguing-in-Publication Data
A catalog record for this book is available from the Library of
Congress

Cover Art by Sarah Pfohl
Cover Design and Typesetting by Ben Stahnke

CONTENTS

INTRODUCTION

_____

FROM "I WILL" TO "I CAN":
THE POLITICAL AND PEDAGOGICAL PLAYFULNESS OF
TYSON E. LEWIS

Derek R. Ford

Having the chance to introduce the thinking (and talking) of Tyson E. Lewis to a new audience of revolutionary activists and organizers is exciting and intimidating. It's exciting because this collection of talks, which cover much of his extensive research interests and span more than a decade, is filled with raw materials out of which communists can produce politically timely and incisive educational practices, theories, and experiments. It's intimidating for the same reasons. Instead of writing an introduction, then, I'm going to write three.

TAKE ONE: THE PERSONAL
I want to first introduce Lewis as a human being, a bundle of atoms and energy holding in place for the time being. I met Lewis in 2013, when I was a graduate student at Syracuse

University and Lewis was an associate professor at Montclair University. I had just reviewed his book, *On Study*, for a journal, and was waiting for his response to it. A few months later, we spoke on a panel about the book at the annual meeting of the Philosophy of Education Society conference in New Mexico, which was the first time we met in person. I was a terrible student in college and most of my primary and secondary schooling (one semester in college I earned a 0.46 GPA), but I *loved* ideas and thinking with others. After some time working and organizing, I enrolled in a graduate course to test the waters, before ending up in SU's cultural foundations of education program totally haphazardly and without any knowledge of education. I was probably annoying my first year in the program because I thought I had something to *prove* to the world. I think I had the same disposition when reviewing Lewis' book, which might be one reason why I ended with a comradely-phrased and, I think, warranted critique about the political implications of the project. In academia, this is a risky move, but it paid off.

Beginning with his responses, Lewis interpellated me as a serious thinker, educator, and organizer and inaugurated a friendship that continues to this day, a friendship that is personal, educational, professional, and political; that is to say, Lewis is a pal and teacher, a colleague and comrade. In each of these roles it's evident that Lewis doesn't only *write* about resisting the capitalist demands of performativity, but he truly practices them. He is uniquely playful, so full of play it's contagious. As he and Richard Kahn put it in their first book, *Education out of Bounds*, "in play, the child's relationship with toys troubles the very distinctions between the proper and the improper," occurring in "a zone of indistinction" that *moves* educational life outside of capital.[1] His research and writing are experimental and sometimes goofy, his lifestyle choices could easily be read as eccentric and lighthearted, his teaching is comical and cheerful, and his politics are always in joyous motion. In these talks, each the play of the friend, teacher, coworker, and comrade comes through as Lewis quotes The Dude from *The Big Lebowski* to crystallize his theory of curiosity as distracted yielding, as he arranges materials for the educational encounter, or as he formulates the reasons why teachers should be ignorant.

For some of my comrades, the relentlessly playful nature of research and teaching might be frustrating or disappointing. It was when I first read his work. When I reviewed *On Study*, I expressed concern about the radical openness of studying, stating that closures will happen sooner or later, and without proposing any answers ourselves we leave it up to the state and capital to provide them. Interestingly, Lewis addressed this provocation at the end of his review response, but he did so in an inconclusive way that merely postponed any definitive thesis and kept the question subject to study. Providing a clear answer as if it was a debate would be to adhere to capital's demand for constant actualization and articulation and would prematurely shut down future collective endeavors, enclosing us off from one another.[2]

---

1   Tyson E. Lewis and Richard Kahn, *Education out of Bounds: Reimagining Cultural Studies for a Posthuman Age* (New York: Palgrave Macmillan, 2010), 70, 71.

2   Lewis even wrote an insightful foreword to my first book, which included a similar critique of his work on studying. See Tyson E. Lewis, "Toward a Communist Philosophy of Education: Reflections on

One political principle sustaining Lewis' work is the united front. When forming united fronts, progressives and communists recognize that they hold important and, in some cases, irreconcilable political differences and acknowledge that those differences shouldn't immediately equate to division. The united front, as Brian Becker writes, "is designed to maximize the participation of the largest number of people in the streets, in the struggle together against imperialism. The political struggle over strategy and orientation will continue—and continue without end—but this united front concept establishes the need to mobilize rather than fragment."[3] Instead of enlarging people in the streets, Lewis expands the number of potential allies in acts of education and, in doing so, demonstrates the humility that's so missing in academia. The arrogant can't rally the masses together, and what allows Lewis to constantly work with new friends and comrades, to bring in new theories and topics, is his openness to external forces working through him and his intentional absent-mindedness, both of which enable him to resist the drive for assessment and evaluation and keep his work and practices continually exposed to contingency.

Take Two: The Pedagogical

We've all heard in classrooms or conferences or read in books or feedback that some aspect of the work needs to be "complicated." About 10 years ago, marxist geographer Don Mitchell heard enough of that, and wrote a brief editorial

Method and Methodology," in D.R. Ford, *Communist Study: Education for the Commons* (Lanham: Lexington Books, 2016).

3   Brian Becker, "Raising Consciousness in the Anti-War Movement," *Liberation School*, 01 May 2006.

against the demand to "complicate" our research, noting that "as an academic cure-all, it's quite simplistic. It's a total fetish." More than that, it's a betrayal of the academic discipline itself, as "complicating" our research does the very opposite of what we're supposed to do. The world in which we research and intervene *is already* complicated, and as such, "the imperative is all the greater that our analyses of it not be, that instead they be clear and incisive."[4]

Importantly, Mitchell's argument was not to rid research of discipline-specific words (i.e., jargon) because such language enables the production of new thought and insights. Instead, his argument was that our expositions should be clear so that we can both enunciate and act in the world, that we should ask each other to think more *critically* about our research and to explain it with greater *precision* rather than asking each other to "complicate" it. I want to propose that Lewis is an example of one who not only explains their own ideas about our incomprehensible world, but also articulates and translates the ideas of others, granting their concepts greater clarity.

Without treading lightly and without any fear of entering the thick weeds of some philosophical thinkers, Lewis has developed a way of not only making remarkably specific ideas and lineages comprehensible, but of making them *come alive* and, even more importantly, making them *educational* and *political*. He's expended an enormous amount of labor doing the hard work of *translating* incredibly dense and complicated theoretical works into educational and political life. This isn't to say that the speeches in this book are exactly *effortless* or

4   Don Mitchell, "A Complicated Fetish," *Social & Cultural Geography* 15, no. 2 (2014): 125.

transparent; they demand care, attention, and persistence. But he leaves clear markers of his theoretical journeys ("first," "second," and "third," or "before we move on, we have to establish X"). He fleshes out his concepts with illustrations that animate the theories and make them accessible.

TAKE THREE: THE POLITICAL

Jacques Rancière's first major book publication is *Althusser's Lesson*. Released in 1974, the book is a sustained critique of his former teacher, Louis Althusser. Rancière's target is not so much Althusser as it is his intellectual project and the methods and strategies used to carry it out. Althusser's pedagogical practice is one where the teacher's role "is to transmit knowledge to those who do not possess it," a principle "founded only on the technical division of labor" between the student and professor.[5] Althusser was, for Rancière, the epitome of a "philosopher king," or what he'd later call the stultifying pedagogue who begins by assuming an inequality between the teacher and student, repressing the latter's capacities by "transmit[ing] his knowledge to his students so as to bring them, by degrees, to his own level of expertise."[6]

Lewis' first single-authored book was on Rancière (and Freire), although there is a more fundamental commonality between the two. A few years after finishing his graduate studies at the University of California Los Angeles, Lewis published a seething critique of a set of books his former teacher,

---

5   Jacques Rancière, *Althusser's Lesson*, trans. E. Battista (New York: Continuum, 2011), 144.

6   Jacques Rancière, *The Ignorant Schoolmaster: Five Lessons in Intellectual Emancipation* (Stanford: Stanford University Press, 1991), 3.

Peter McLaren, published in 2005-2006. Like Rancière, Lewis' sights aren't set on McLaren as a person; unlike Rancière, they aren't set on McLaren as a teacher. Instead, Lewis proposes an "immanent critique" of McLaren's work, highlighting internal contradictions within the three primary aspects of McLaren's project. First, McLaren's project entails *reason* that reintroduces class analysis within education to correct for the domesticated versions of critical pedagogy that abandon the revolutionary project. By doing so, the second domain of *revolution* enters, as McLaren envisions an educational practice that produces revolutionary consciousness through critique, in which "education and revolution have to be fused together."[7] In other words, pedagogy is marginally considered or "eternally deferred" as there are neither any classroom translations nor examples to move from the abstract to the particular.

For Lewis, "the dearth of examples indicates a *theoretical* error in McLaren's project, muting his clarion call to form a 'philosophy of praxis' through which action and theory interpenetrate one another." In their place, we have "dozens of manifestos that do not realise Marx's own plea for a new sense of action."[8] This leads to the third and most damning critique of McLaren's *passion*: revolutionary critical pedagogy is a philosophy rather than a pedagogy, as he and his co-thinkers at the time were working to recenter the educational problematic within marxism (without expanding it out anymore).

---

7   Tyson E. Lewis, "Capitalists and Conquerors Teaching Against Global Capitalism and the New Imperialism Rage and Hope: Interviews with Peter McLaren on War, Imperialism, and Critical Pedagogy," *Historical Materialism* 17, no. 1 (2009): 202.

8   Ibid., 204.

McLaren's passion is the most redeeming for Lewis. This is evidenced in McLaren's writing style that is characterized by a "poetic quality," an attribute of his writing that can make room for "a new aesthetic level of vision for re-imagining political life beyond the current distribution of the sensible."[9] Lewis concludes that McLaren's project has as many aporias as it does answers, and that McLaren can't finish developing his revolutionary critical pedagogy so long as he merely imported marxism into educational theory. Instead, the task of revolutionary pedagogies is to "transform Marxist theory through this articulation" of pedagogical theory in a "dialectical movement between pedagogy and theory."[10]

Lewis continued interrogating his former teacher with another paper published in 2010, in which he figures McLaren (and Giroux) as a prophet of "apocalyptic" pedagogy," an educational understanding and presentation of time as "the end of time, poised between 'ontological terror' from the right and the absolute necessity of revolution from the left."[11] The target here is McLaren's pedagogy of the manifestos, which "dictate proper political action and proper political goals in light of historical necessity and an impending world crisis."[12] Lewis proposes it's plagued by two key problems. The first is that, by structuring it around the endpoint of the great class war, McLaren neglects a more nuanced conception of struggle articulated by Marx. The second is that the introduction of

9   Ibid., 206, 207.

10   Ibid., 207.

11   Tyson E. Lewis, "Messianic Pedagogy," *Educational Theory* 60, no. 2 (2010): 243.

12   Ibid., 244.

marxist-humanism (via Hegel) prevents revolutionary critical pedagogy from the revolutionary potential of the *surplus present* of the now.

If Rancière had to settle accounts with Althusser early in his career, then Lewis had to do the same with McLaren. It caused a fallout between the two of them just before I started my own graduate studies. When I entered Syracuse University in 2012, I was already a long-time marxist and Party member. I investigated marxism and education and, of course, quickly found McLaren's prolific body of work, along with that of Dave Hill, Glen Rikowski, Paula Allman, Sandy Grande, and others. It was incredibly helpful and provided the first time for me to get a "footing" in an entirely new field. At the same time, I was looking for something that would better address the specifically *pedagogical* elements of marxism, revolutionary struggle, and communist organization.

This brought me to Lewis' work, in his 2012 paper "Mapping the Constellations of Educational Marxism(s)" and his 2013 book, *On Study*. His 2012 paper characterized educational marxisms around three domains: knowledge and epistemology (consciousness raising), education for political persuasion to build hegemony, and an ontological project to constitute a new political body. This is where I first learned that Paulo Freire constructed his *Pedagogy of the Oppressed* "as a tool to be used within revolutionary organization to mediate the various relationships between the oppressed and the leaders of resistance" and positioned it as a response to or development on Georg Lukacs' work.[13] More importantly, I ex-

---

13   Tyson E. Lewis, "Mapping the Constellation of Educational Marxism(s)," *Educational Philosophy and Theory* 44, no. S1 (2012): 102.

perienced Lewis' nascent methodology for writing educational philosophy.

The cartographic project doesn't privilege or denounce any domain but argues we need to discern the differences between the registers and ultimately utilize them all through a constellational method. Taking a constellational approach enables each domain to enrich the others through their differences but "does not resolve tensions within and between competing theories, but rather realizes that such tensions are productive indexes that both connect and disconnect singular theoretical registers."[14]

This might be Lewis' first stab at a marxist *pedagogy of praxis*: education is the navigation of different registers in marxist educational theory via constellational thinking, which "does not collapse differences between concepts, nor does it simply valorize one conceptual model over the other. Rather they hang precariously together, maintaining an absent center."[15] As Lewis says in the opening to his first talk, his research maps interruptions in dominant forms of educational life and, I'd add, develops new concepts and practices that disrupt the ontology of effectiveness to resist the demand for operativity, dwelling instead in the aporias and gaps of study.

The pedagogy of studying as an alternative educational mode to the domination of learning seemed to be in the air, as Lewis's book *On Study* appeared the same year as Stefano Harney and Fred Moten's work on Black study, *The Undercommons*. Lewis's book was the culmination of a decade or so of working with Giorgio Agamben's philosophy to rethink

14   Ibid., 99.

15   Ibid., 112.

the most fundamental axioms of educational philosophy and practice. His first paper on the topic was rejected from numerous journals, and it took him several years to finally find an outlet for it. We should all be glad he persisted, because I deeply believe the groundwork he lays there is absolutely crucial in the educational dynamics of the revolutionary class struggle. It's there that he proposes learning is the pedagogical motor of biocapitalism, and to do so he deploys what I read as his unique educational and philosophical methodology: listening to the pedagogical silences of the world and letting them speak through him.

For those subjects worthy of investment, "biocapitalism [...] does not depreciate or use-up one's labor power so much as continually invests in the production and reproduction of such power through a total integration of one's potentiality into an economic/learning structure that emphasizes continual reskilling in order to survive within competitive global markets."[16] Rather than examining the political contradictions or possibilities of biocapitalism as an economic, political, and social system, Lewis hears its underlying pedagogical motor: learning. Learning is the movement from ignorance to mastery, from inability to ability, or "the putting to work of potentiality in the name of self-actualization and economic viability."[17] He spends as much time conceptualizing learning as he does alternative logics that divorce potentiality from the demand to actualize. Remaining within potentiality isn't to inhabit a state of inactivity or impotence, but rather an ambivalent dis-

---

16   Lewis, *On Study: Giorgio Agamben and Educational Potentiality* (New York: Routledge, 2013), 3-4.

17   Ibid., 5.

position in which everything is possible. If learning is about "I will" then study is about "I can." As he writes in chapter 8, "To say 'I can' is a strange act. It is a kind of happening where nothing happens, or a happening in which nothing happens except the potentiality for happening." Because "I can" is only a potentiality, it can't be assessed or measured, evaluated or graded, judged or employed.

This is a book that repeatedly says, "I can," in different languages and settings, through different voices and characters, but for a united cause: the study of that which capital can't exploit, oppress, or enclose. Before reading his voice on your own, I want to leave you with a final comment. Lewis and I do share a common political and educational objective, which is to experiment with and propose pedagogical theories and practices to enable us and others to *experience* an alternative educational form of life beyond learning and capitalism. In place of critiques of educational systems and processes, I've taken Lewis' lead in focusing on how to generate the experience of a revolutionary alternative present in the now of the classroom and library, the union hall and street demonstration, the bus stop and the playground.

PART I

A CONSTELLATION OF
EDUCATIONAL PRACTICES

CHAPTER 1

THINKING EDUCATION OUT OF BOUNDS

Often, I am asked to clarify how my work "fits together."[1] Am I building a system with a coherent and consistent logic? Or is something else at stake in the various concepts and practices I have put forward over the years? What is the "through line" that unites all the disparate elements of my work, or are all my essays and books merely a dispersed rhizome without a center?

I must admit that systems do not interest me very much. Instead, I have always concerned myself with mapping various interruptions, suspensions, or even explosions of dominant educational trends, or educational forms of "common sense." This might mean reassessing supposedly anti-educational concepts such as "stupidity" or "ignorance" or "distraction." Or it might be privileging marginal or obscure educational figures,

---

1   This manuscript was part of an interview conducted by Steve Valk and Alexander Strecker for the Social Choreography Lab at Duke University. The interview took place on April 26, 2021.

such as the liminal studier who is often overshadowed by the figure of the learner.[2] Or it might be in terms of inventing new educational practices, such as exopedagogy.[3] All in all, what these tendrils have in common is a fundamental gesture of refusal, a "preferring not to" abide by restrictions placed on the who, what, when, where, and how of educational discourse and practice. Each practice can, in turn, be loosely grouped and regrouped according to a constellational method (rather than a system), or a method that is open-ended, dynamic, and oscillating, each element in the constellation taking on slightly different valences through its tactical position.[4]

Take for instance my first attempt to destabilize humanist educational discourses: exopedagogy. Exopedagogy was an educational articulation of the political category of exodus, most famously theorized by proponents of autonomist Marxism. For Italian Marxists, exodus is a form of creative refusal to labor under capitalist conditions of production in order to create new forms of life.[5] In education, this type of exodus would involve several different types of refusals:

1) A refusal to view education as an economic transaction. Today, we can see this economic understanding of

2   Lewis, *On Study,* and Tyson E. Lewis, *Inoperative Learning: A Radical Rewriting of Educational Potentialities* (New York: Routledge, 2017).

3   Lewis and Kahn, *Education Out of Bounds.*

4   Lewis, "Mapping the Constellation of Educational Marxism(s)." Indeed, this current book is one such constellation of pedagogical practices and theories.

5   Michael Hardt and Antonio Negri, *Empire* (Cambridge, MA: Harvard University Press, 2000), 212.

education in many ways. First, education is seen as an investment in the future of the individual and society. Second, such investment demands taking on certain debts. The language of investment and debt were so easily imported into education discourse precisely because learning itself is predicated on a certain economic management of student and teacher relationships.[6] This makes learning amenable to capitalist co-optation. So, exopedagogy would have to be a non-economistic understanding of education—an ecological alternative.

2) A refusal to create a humanist education that is based on a fundamental division between forms of life that ultimately ends up privileging the human. Walter Benjamin once said that the aim of education in the West is to produce the human citizen.[7] To do so, that which is other-than-human has to be devalued and perhaps sacrificed.[8] If this is the case, there is a fundamental violence at the heart of the humanist notion of education in the sense that an investment into the production of the human necessitates an exclusion of that which is labeled as unhuman or inhuman (including non-human animals, but also non-Western peoples, slaves, and women). Thus, exopedagogy would have to be some kind of posthumanist

---

6   Gert Biesta refers to this as "learnification." See Biesta, *Beyond Learning: Democratic Education for a Human Future* (Boulder: Paradigm Publishers, 2006).

7   Walter Benjamin, *Selected Writings, Volume 2, Part 1, 1927-1930*, eds. M.W. Jennings, H. Eiland, G. Smith (Cambridge, MA: The Belknap Press of Harvard University Press, 2005), 273.

8   Lewis, *Inoperative Learning*, Chapter 4 and Interruption 4.

educational practice, one that refuses any kind of anthropocentric hierarchy that would divide life against itself.[9]

3) A refusal to remain in place as either a public or private good. For so long, education has been seen as either property of the state or private interests, and the war has been to preserve public education against privatization or corporatization. Yet this language of private vs. public seems to miss other forms of informal, nontraditional schooling that fall out of bounds of this dichotomy, this would be the domain of exopedagogical practices found in social movements, aesthetic experiments, subcultures, or the "undercommons" of various institutions.[10] Exopedagogy turns its attention to other places besides schools to investigate pedagogies that are unprofessional and unsanctioned by the state or for-profit corporations.

So, the goal of my first book, *Education Out of Bounds*, was an attempt to formulate exopedagogy not simply as a critique of institutionalized, humanist, capitalist learning but more importantly as a positive and productive practice of forming other kinds of educational life that are ecologically grounded, aesthetically experimental, and utopic (or atopic, as the case

---

9   For an example of posthumanist, exopedagogical politics, see Tyson E. Lewis, "Swarm Intelligence: Rethinking the Multitude from within the Transversal Commons," *Culture, Theory, and Critique* 51, no. 3: 223-238.

10   See Tyson E. Lewis, "Exopedagogy: On Pirates, Shorelines, and the Educational Commonwealth," *Educational Philosophy and Theory* 44, no. 8 (2012): 845-861. And for undercommons, see Stefano Harney and Fred Moten, *The Undercommons: Fugitive Planning & Black Study* (New York: Minor Compositions, 2013).

might be). This would be a monstrous education, meaning an education that does not abide by the rules of what education ought to produce, where education ought to occur, or whom education ought to involve.

My co-author, Richard Kahn, and I turned for inspiration to a rather odd set of subcultures and countercultures to see if they contained exopedagogical dimensions. In particular, we looked at reptoid conspiracy theories, faerie faiths, and zoophilic practices. While all three were problematic in their own ways, we also found that in each case there were elements of exopedagogical practices that we might describe as follows:

1) Schooling takes place out of bounds of capitalist economic relationships and attempts to undo the sacrifice of humanist logics to create new kinds of ecologically open forms of life. These would be forms of life that do not exploit or view the other-than-human as either that which must be sacrificed or turned into a resource.

2) They attempt to inspire posthuman ecologies through an intensification and expansion of what we called the savage and zoomorphic dimensions of the imagination. Drawing on Antonio Negri's work, we define the savage imagination as a critique of Power inequalities and social hierarchies in the name of multitudinous constituting powers from below.[11] And the zoomorphic dimension of the imagination critiques the anthropocentrism of humanism to return the human to its exiled animality. This allows the animal, the body, the instincts, preconscious

11 Antonio Negri, *The Savage Anomaly*, trans. M. Hardt (Minneapolis: University of Minnesota Press, 1991).

sensations to speak, and to "teach" lessons to the humanist subject.

3) Exopedagogy ignites and intensifies both the savage and zoomorphic dimensions of the imagination by reconceptualizing curriculum as a bestiary of monsters. Our book, *Education Out of Bounds*, was one such bestiary, turning to contemporary forms of the monstrous to organize them into progressive and regressive categories.

4) The goal would be to create a theory and practice of common education: one that is not economically exclusive so much as ecologically inclusive of human and other-than-human actors. No longer would education be a technology for either repressing the monstrous within or projecting the monstrous onto the outside world, instead exopedagogy would be a creatively critical literacy of the monster and of monstrous practices.

Speaking of monsters and contamination today might seem rather in poor taste. COVID-19 has made us all aware of how fragile the human is to other-than-human forms of life, revealing the vulnerability of Power to economically organize the management of populations. But the educational responses to COVID-19 speak to certain limitations in our imagination. For instance, there are those who argue to stay at home to prevent contamination. This is a kind of retreat into the illusion of the humanist home as a pure, sanitized, safe harbor from difference.[12]

---

12   For an analysis of the home in literature, film, and philosophy, see Tyson E. Lewis and Daniel Cho, "Home is Where the Neurosis Is: A Topography of the Spatial Unconscious," *Cultural Critique* 64, Fall

On the other hand, you have politicians arguing that schools must open again so that students can learn to be good, productive, efficient human citizens and that adults can return to their jobs. I would say that both perspectives lack both savage and zoomorphic dimensions. What would an exopedagogical response to COVID-19 be? Here I would like to turn to a recent article I published on the re-wilding of urban spaces during the early days of the pandemic.[13] As humans fled inside, a host of wildlife took over largely human urban centers. It is my suggestion that a new kind of exopedagogy could have emerged from this crossing of speciesist boundaries, creating a new kind of educational bestiary that exists when humans and more-than-human others mingle. The lessons learned from such contamination of urban spaces might concern a new ecological awareness of who shares what resources and who has the right to the city. It might prompt a rethinking of a common city that accommodates human and more-than-human actors. This perspective would not cast COVID-19 as merely an obstacle to getting back to work, but as an opportunity for seeing social distancing as opening up to new forms of ecological intimacy.

Study

My theory of study is also another alternative to economized, humanist educational philosophy and practice. It is another type of education out of bounds:

(2005): 69-91.

13 Tyson E. Lewis, "Cities Gone Wild," *Postdigital Science and Education* 2 (2020): 597-600.

1) To distinguish learning from studying, we can turn to Vilém Flusser's theory of gestures.[14] For Flusser, there are essentially 4 kinds of gestures. Using his distinctions, I argue that learning is work and communication whereas study is disinterested and ritualistic.[15] What does this mean? A gesture of work is one that produces material manifestations of itself, and a gesture of communication is oriented toward others. In relation to learning, we can see how learning produces works (literally homework), and the function of this work is to communicate development, growth, or progress to another (usually the teacher). Studying is different. It is a disinterested gesture, meaning it is disinterested in achieving the kinds of ends that concern learning. In this sense, it can appear to be unproductive from the point of view of learning. And studying is a ritualistic gesture in that its structure is circular and rather unpractical. The studier returns to the same texts repeatedly. Instead of learning, which is like an arrow, directed at outcomes and ends, the studier is interested in constantly returning to the means of thinking. He or she is interested in the means as such. Like all rituals, this means that studying is an unpractical practice. It does not concern growth, development, or progress.

2) The location of study is also unique. Predominantly, learning is situated within the bounds of the school where

14   Vilém Flusser, *Gestures*, trans. Nancy Ann Roth (Minneapolis: University of Minnesota Press, 2014).

15   Tyson E. Lewis, "Study: A Disinterested Passion," in ed. D. Ford, *Keywords in Radical Philosophy and Education: Common Concepts for Contemporary Movements* (Leiden: Brill, 2019).

it can be overseen and directed by the teacher and evaluated according to external criteria of excellence and achievement. Yet, study often happens in the studio or studiolo. In the studio, the studier can get lost in thought, experiment with ideas, create generative protocols (tiny rituals) for him or herself. It is an a-disciplinary space, existing before the compartmentalization and specialization of the disciplines. Finally, the studio is an ambiguous space that is neither fully inside nor outside traditional households or institutions. It is adjacent to the economy of household management or classroom instruction.[16]

3) The study that takes place in the studio is also monstrous, meaning it transgresses certain boundaries, certain definitions of the proper vs. the improper. For instance, study often is depicted as taking place at night when we are supposed to be asleep replenishing our labor power so we can be productive in the morning. Study is also often described as an addiction. It is unproductive activity that perpetuates itself at the expense of more useful and pragmatic forms of labor. This addiction happens at night, and as such is a special kind of nocturnal transformation of the studier according to the light of the moon. It is a lycanthropic educational practice. Just as the moon's effects on the earth involve the repetition of the tides, so too the gesture of study is a rhythmic, circling activity.

4) Finally, learning privileges actualization over potentialization whereas study emphasizes potentialization.

16   Tyson E. Lewis and Peter Hyland, *Studious Drift: Movements and Protocols for a Postdigital Education* (Minneapolis: University of Minnesota Press, 2022).

This is not a retreat into pure potentiality. It is instead an attempt to think a form of actualization that does not sacrifice or exhaust potentiality but rather exhibits or embodies it. For instance, in learning, one has an intention that is externalized as a work that communicates growth, development, or progress. As such, learning privileges the actualization of a potentiality as a final cause. Yet in study, there is an interest in exploring means without orienting the means toward a final cause or a specific, predetermined end. This opens up study to the possibility of not simply employing one's potentiality to achieve an end, but of experiencing one's potentiality as such. In this sense, the greatest discovery of study is not what one can do in the form of an achievement but rather the discovery that one can do something, that one's potentiality is finally revealed to oneself.[17]

Aesthetics of Education

Underlying these diverse projects is a consistent interest in aesthetics. The "aesthetics of education" as a phrase is meant to indicate that education first and foremost is a certain activity that affects what can and cannot be seen, heard, smelled, tasted, and so forth. It fundamentally challenges the partitioning of the sensible, as Rancière would say.[18] Throughout my many projects, I have been struggling to express this fundamental idea in various ways. In my first book *Education Out of*

---

17   Tyson E. Lewis, "Education for Potentiality (Against Instrumentality)," *Policy Futures in Education* 18, no. 7 (2020): 878-891.

18   Jacques Rancière, *The Politics of Aesthetics*, trans. G. Rockhill (London: Continuum, 2004).

Bounds, I use posthumanist language and Deleuzian notions of sensation and affect while in my most recent book *Walter Benjamin's Anti-Fascist Education,*[19] I use the notion of inner-vation of bodily energies to convey moments when the body breaks out of fascist rigidification (hardness and coldness). In all cases, what I am after is a sense of education as an embod-ied event that explores what a body can do.

In this expanded sense, I see aesthetics not as a discipline of philosophy or as a practice specific to art education (in the form of aesthetic critique). Instead, I see aesthetics as funda-mental to all forms of education. Learning and studying thus would have their own aesthetics, their own ways in which bodies are affected.

This leads me to choreography. For me, choreography is not about dance per se but rather about an open-ended exper-iment with the composition and decomposition of bodies. It is a redistribution of what bodies can do, where they can do it, and how they can do it. Choreography is the possibility of recalibrating the gravitational relationship between bodies and their worlds, experimenting with the pliability of gestures and movements. It is a way of studying the body, meaning that it is a way of throwing into relief the potentialities of the gestures of the body through unproductive practice that is disinterested in predetermined ends. Choreography can project bodies out beyond the economy of movements that make them recogniz-able and functional within society, creating a new ecology of monstrous bodies that precisely do what they are not supposed to do, appear where they are not supposed to appear.

---

19   Tyson E. Lewis, *Walter Benjamin's Anti-Fascist Education: From Riddles to Radio* (New York: SUNY Press, 2020).

Exopedagogy and study are alternative modes of choreographing educational life, with their own aesthetics (what can be seen, felt, sensed). They are practices of education that expand what counts as an educational gesture and whose bodies are capable of such gestures. In this sense, while my work has diversified over the years, it has remained concerned with this fundamental problematic: How can the choreography of the learner be suspended so that other choreographies of educational bodies can appear?

PART II

RETHINKING THE SUBJECT OF EDUCATION

CHAPTER 2

WHAT IS A MARXIST PHILOSOPHY
OF EDUCATION?

As an Institutional State Apparatus (ISA), the school for French Marxist Louis Althusser produces a subject as an effect of ideological interpellation.[1] Quoting Althusser:

> In other words, the school (but also other State institutions like the Church, or other apparatuses like the Army) teaches 'know-how,' but in forms which ensure subjection to the ruling ideology or the mastery of its 'practice.' All the agents of production, exploitation, and repression, not to speak of the 'professional of ideology' (Marx) must in one way or another be 'steeped' in this ideology to perform their tasks 'consciously.'[2]

Production demands a support function to be occupied by a subject who recognizes him or herself as the performer of that function. It is ideological interpellation that subjectivizes the subject into this support function by granting a "reason-

1   Presented at the American Educational Research Association, 2016, Washington, D.C.

2   Louis Althusser, *Lenin and Philosophy and Other Essays*, trans. B. Brewster (New York: Monthly Review Press, 2001), 89.

to-be-a-subject."[3]

This description is a sound starting point for understanding schooling in capitalist society, but it should not be seen as a prescription for Marxist education. Education in a historical materialist sense is not, I will argue, interpellation into a predefined subject position. While schooling produces a subject of ideology as an act of social reproduction, Marxist education produces something else entirely, something beyond the subject. But what is produced by the practice of education that is distinct from a subject? And here I do not mean a subject of capitalist production, but rather a subject as such, a subject as a bourgeois, humanist concept. But before we can answer this pressing issue, we have to understand what a practice consists of. For Althusser, a practice is a process of transformation of a raw material into a specific product, a transformation effected by a determinate human labor.[4] Thus ideological practice (as carried out by ISAs) is characterized by working over a particular raw material (forms of representation), to create a subject of the state, through the labor of teaching. Political practice on the other hand is characterized by working on social relations to create a new set of social relations through the act of revolution. One produces a citizen subject, the other an activist subject. The question for us becomes: How to delineate education as a specific practice? What are its raw materials, its labor, and its product? What makes something *educational* and not just political? And how does this practice articulate differentially

---

3   Louis Althusser, *The Humanist Controversy and Other Writings*, ed. Francois Matheron (London: Verso, 2003), 51.

4   Louis Althusser, *Philosophy for Non-Philosophers*, trans. G.M. Goshgarian (London: Bloomsbury Press, 2017), 85.

with other practices (politics, ideology, science, etc.)?

There are several obstacles in our way to understanding the practice of education in Althusser's work. First, Althusser's stated theory of teaching is reductive and simplistic. Althusser argues that the function of teaching is "to transmit a determinate knowledge to subjects who do not possess this knowledge. The teaching situation thus rests on the absolute condition of an inequality between a knowledge and a nonknowledge."[5] As such, the question of teaching is reduced to simple transmission of content from the expert subject to the ignorant subject. Althusser's overt comments on teaching seem to define both Althusser's theory of schooling and his comments concerning Marxist education. I would suggest that there are three problems here. First, education remains attached to the bourgeois concept of subjects and subject positions. Second, because education remains at the level of subject formation, it concerns knowledge or know-how, and thus is ideological in nature. It concerns correct ideological orientation or subjection to a counter ideology, this time of a Marxist variety. Indeed, Marxist education would amount to a counter-interpellation: or interpellation of the subject under the sign of Marxist ideology. But how exactly is this different from ideological practice? Third, because ideological knowledge has to be transmitted from subject A (who is supposed to know) to subject B (who is supposed to be lacking), it involves a fundamental inequality. Here we might recall the criticisms of Althusser's student Rancière who argues that "liberatory" education produces

    5   Jacques Rancière, *The Ignorant Schoolmaster: Five Lessons in Intellectual Emancipation*, trans. Kristin Ross (Stanford: Stanford University Press, 1991), xvi.

the very conditions of stultifying inequality that it is meant to overcome.[6] Such inequality is fundamental to the capitalist mode of production which demands submission to a chain of command, leading downward from owners of the means of production to laborers. In short, Althusser's model of education is shot through with bourgeois concepts such as the subject. It is also mired in the "naturalization" of inequality—a condition that adheres to the very heart of capitalist production. Althusser fails to theorize Marxist education as such and rather focuses on Marxist schooling as a form of counter-interpellative practice.[7]

My wager here is that to understand what Marxist education proper is, we must understand Marxist education beyond the humanist emphasis on the subject and on the transference of knowledge, and we have to think education beyond the logic of inequality. This would mean that Marxist education is opposed to Marxist criticisms of schooling. We can find new resources for this in Althusser's late philosophy of the encounter. The essay begins with a simple observation: "It is raining."[8] Rain falling unpredictably from the heavens is in constant motion, moving at different speeds, subject to different forces, and its trajectories are largely unexpected. Rain as it falls becomes the principle example of what Althusser calls "a *materialism of the encounter*, and therefore of the aleatory and of contingen-

---

6   Ibid.

7   See David I. Backer, "Interpellation, Counterinterpellation, and Education," *Critical Education* 9, no. 15 (2018): 1-21.

8   Louis Althusser, *Philosophy of the Encounter: Later Writings 1978-1987*, trans. G.M. Goshgarian (London: Verso, 1993/2006), 167.

cy."[9] According to Epicurus's metaphysics, at the origin of the world, there existed only atoms falling parallel to one another inside of a void. Then, unexpectedly a clinamen intervenes producing an "infinitesimal *swerve*"[10] that ruptures the orderly parallel distribution of atoms. A series of encounters akin to a chain reaction occurs because of this swerve effect leading to the birth of the world. What is important to note in this reading is that (a) the swerve is not created by Reason or by the agency of a subject, (b) it cannot be predicted in advance by any knowledge system, and (c) the product is not a subject but rather a world, which is the precondition for new subjectivities. There is no intentionality behind the swerve, nor any line of inquiry that can be traced back to its ultimate Cause. And the appearance of the swerve cannot be predicated on any agency. In fact, no explanation can be given for its arrival, and no formula can be devised for its increasingly complex set of overdetermined effects, nor can any formula be generated to predict its appearance.

What is the role of philosophy in this materialism of the encounter? Simply put, it is to verify the existence of contingency, of aleatory encounters as such. Here Althusser points to Machiavelli as an exemplar. Machiavelli's thought concerns the conditions for inducing a certain swerve effect to unify Italy. Yet his conclusions are shocking: "[...] unification will be achieved if there emerges some nameless man who has enough luck and *virtù* to establish himself somewhere, in some *nameless* corner of Italy, and, starting out from this atomic point, gradually aggregate the Italians around him in the grand proj-

---

9   Ibid.

10   Ibid.

ect of founding a national state."[11] As Althusser summarizes, "This is a completely aleatory line of reasoning, which leaves politically *blank* both the name of the Federator and that of the region which will serve as starting point for the constitution of this federation."[12] In other words, a void is posited, but this void is not fixed to this or that location in the order of things, and will only appear in a nameless and contingent place.

The answer given by Machiavelli is not an answer that presupposes the mastery of the teacher who is supposed to know, but rather the philosopher who is ignorant but attentive to the sudden appearance of an unknown man (someone without a name, and thus without a position within the order of things) in an unassignable place (outside any ideologically bound territories), and thus awaits an encounter that may or may not happen given the contingency of elements necessary to produce the swerve effect, the results of which—"gigantic pile-up and collision-interlocking"[13] atoms—constitute the world. In a sweeping gesture that stakes out a new materialist horizon for understanding contemporary thought, Althusser summarizes "We shall say, then, that the materialism of the encounter is contained in the thesis of the primacy of positivity over negativity (Deleuze), the thesis of the primacy of the swerve over the rectilinearity of the straight trajectory (the Origin is a swerve from it, not the reason for it), the thesis of the primacy of 'dissemination' over the postulate that every signifier has a meaning (Derrida), and in the welling up of order from the

11   Ibid., 172.

12   Ibid.

13   Ibid., 191.

very heart of disorder to produce a world."[14]

The philosopher is the one who is *sensitive* to the situation in which contingent elements—atoms independent of one another—collide with one another through the induction of non-teleological swerve effect to produce a certain world (a world that has no necessity and thus could have been different). In other words, the aleatory encounter is precisely (a) an encounter between nameless atoms, (b) a field of force relations rather than knowledge relations, (c) a radical equality of all elements, any one of which can set off a swerve effect at any given time, and (d) presupposes divergence and disorientation rather than convergence and orientation. This is *not* a linear experience wherein one hears a call, turns toward the call, and is thereby interpellated into a predetermined subject position. Rather it is an experience of falling offline, of colliding, of spiraling outward into an unknown subject position. It is my argument that Marxist education is a practice of encountering.

In conclusion, I would argue that Marxist education is a practice (a) whose raw materials are the constituent elements of the subject (imaginary, affective, and symbolic), (b) whose practice is the encounter (a clash between such elements that causes a swerve effect in the subject), and (c) whose product is a subject without a subject (a subject estranged from itself, a de-subjectivized subject). Education is not simply an educational interpellation or counter-interpellation because it does not concern itself with mirror-recognition ("Yes, that is the kind of subject I am!") but rather with the possibility of dis-interpellation that makes the subject unfamiliar to itself, and thus open to its own dissolution. Since the swerve of the

---

14   Ibid., 189-190.

encounter is never predictable and never reducible to the Reason of the teacher, it is something that emerges *from the clash of atoms (students, teachers, curricula, various historical contingencies, etc.).* It is an unpredictable eruption wherein a fundamental equality is enacted in the sense that no one controls it, no one has particular rights over interpreting it, and no one can predict its outcomes.

For this reason, the aleatory teacher cannot orient the student toward proper knowledge but rather, like the materialist philosopher, should function to verify the swerve effect produced by the clash of atoms. The swerve and encounter cannot be predicted or planned. They are not brought about but rather *happen.* In other words, the role of the aleatory teacher is to bear witness to the dissolution of the markers of subjectivity, and thus the void of dis-interpellation as an opening to another way of thinking, to the very possibility for thinking something anew. Instead of repressing such moments of disorientation, such a teacher *holds onto them and thus plunges into the void with the student.* It is only through this gesture that a *new* kind of educational world opens through which a different kind of subject than that which is expected might emerge.

Whereas most Marxist educators are theorists of the school, and thus are concerned with the production of subjects to support a particular ideological imaginary, I am arguing for a different kind of Marxist educational practice that is aleatory, open to the unpredictable and destabilizing contingencies of the historical conjuncture of atoms, and thus concerns forces rather than subjects, equality rather than inequality, and is decisively anti-humanist, open-ended, and materialist through and through.

But how is this Marxist? It is important at this point to end with a reminder that for Althusser, there is no subject of history. The proletarian class is *not* a subject but a force that clashes and swerves in unpredictable ways and at unforeseen times (the critical conjunction in the overdetermined structure of social relations is, at best, only seen in retrospect). As such, an education through de-subjectification is part of a broader Marxist agenda, for it is only in the abrupt collapse of the bourgeois sense of the subject that one can touch (however obliquely) a communist horizon—not as a subjective disposition or even a desire but rather as a *force* that emerges from a clash of elements. Without de-subjectification as an educational moment, then it would be all too easy to reinscribe humanist notions of the subject back into the class struggle (as is often the case with Marxist humanists). The problem here is how ideological orientation wins out over and against materialist disorientation, and how subjective interpellation wins out over and against materialist dis-interpellation.

In short, the aleatory teacher is one who bears witness and maintains the clash of atoms when the swerve occurs. The aleatory student is the one who suffers the effects of the swerve on subjectivity. It is in this way that the Marxist educational subject is a subject without a subject, a no one, an anonymous and unknown man/woman without a name, a force that is open to a new kind of world, a communist world.[15]

---

15   See, for example, Derek R. Ford, *Communist Study: Education for the Commons,* 2nd. ed. (Lanham: Lexington Books, 2022).

CHAPTER 3

IMPERSONAL EDUCATION AND
THE COMMONS

The language of personhood seems to permeate our educational landscape.[1] Thus, it is not uncommon today to
hear advocates of the privatization of public education speak
about the liberal ideals of personal choice, individual rights,
and privately owned property. Interestingly, those on the far
right also speak about personhood education as an alternative to comprehensive sex education. Progressive parents, on
the other hand, seek teachers that let their children develop
into full persons, teachers who can make personal accommo-
dations to the uniqueness of each singular child, and teachers
who allow children to express their personalities, and so forth.
From liberal to conservative camps, the language of the person
fundamentally shapes the landscape of learning.

And if this is indeed an accurate set of assumptions, so

---

1   This paper was delivered at the American Educational Research Association conference in San Antonio, TX in 2017.

what? One can quickly point to the political importance of the concept of personhood for extending rights beyond White, male, property-owning, adult citizens. Between the figure of bare life which has no legal status and the citizen (who is granted rights by the nation-state) stands the person, who is defined by the right to bear rights that are universally granted simply by the fact that one is a person (regardless of class, race, gender, nationality and so forth). If there are current problems with human rights (including the problems related to the rights of refugees), then these problems concern how such rights are enforced and who is considered a person. Within a liberal paradigm, the notion of personhood itself is never to blame for such problems. The goal is simply to expand who counts as a person.

Yet Roberto Esposito argues that the real problem facing politics today is not an improvement of the correspondence between rights and persons so much as the figure of the person as such.[2] For Esposito, the very concept is problematic. At its base, personhood divides life against itself, and is thus part of what he terms an immunological paradigm that splits the body from the mind, the rational and the animal, the inside and the outside, the self from the other. This immunological paradigm includes (a) liberal forms of personhood as ownership, (b) religious fundamentalist forms of pro-life personhood, and (c) fascist attempts to politicize personhood in the name of national health. Underlying every manifestation is the submission of biological life/the body to the level of a thing to be owned, managed, or destroyed. In short there is a dialectic

---

2   Roberto Esposito, *Third Person*, trans. Z. Hanafi (Cambridge: Polity Press, 2012).

between personalization and depersonalization/animalization that continually inscribes itself in Western approaches to politics and law. If this is the case on the political level, then we also need to question the unexamined consequences that draw together learning and personhood as an unquestioned educational good.

For Esposito, the alternative is a shift from the personal to the impersonal, thus recuperating that which would otherwise be sacrificed (the body, the outside, the other). If Esposito's question concerns the question of a politically impersonal life, my question could be phrased in educational terms as: What would it mean to lead an impersonal educational life? While learning to be a person, personal learning, and learning as personhood all equate education with individual ownership, personal advancement, and/or self-actualization, an impersonal education would return education back to the commonwealth, back to what is held in common. Rather than an immunizing education through learning, what we have is an affirmative bio-political education for impersonal flourishing.

In short, while other papers on this panel have discussed the social dimensions of the commons, what I would like to do is argue that the commons is not only something that is external but also something that is radically internal as well: that which is most anonymous, that which is most disavowed, that which is most impersonal within the person is precisely an excess that cannot be owned, managed, and/or reduced to a specific form of subjectivity within the order of things. This impersonal kernel is precisely how the commons comes to define us not in terms of where we are or what we do so much as who we are.

I am most concerned in this short paper with how legal discourse situates the child in relation to this dialectic between personalization and depersonalization. Here is but one example: Dame Justice Elizabeth Butler-Sloss's statement that the "child is a person." What is striking about this statement is twofold. First, it is striking that Butler-Sloss felt compelled to formulate an argument for this position. In other words, it is not self-evident that children are full-fledged persons. Second, despite support for this claim, there are many who argue that Butler-Sloss's clarion call has not been adequately heard in the United States. Caroline Sawyer points out that the limited personhood of the child is directly related to the restriction in children's legal rights to questions pertaining to family law.[3] Within the scope of family law the child is conceptualized as dependent on the family, and his or her legal rights are reduced to the single right to *not* have the state interfere with the private family (unless the child's welfare is at stake). Lacking any positive, autonomous legal status, a child alone is conceptualized as somehow pathological or disabled. Sawyer argues that the result has been the subjugation of children.

As an alternative, Sawyer makes the claim that "Children would be more appropriately regarded not as dependent family members but as social actors, as in the social sciences literature. Their childhood should not mean their exclusion from the legal fabric. Instead, it should entitle them to a legal personality that accommodates their youth, as can be seen in oth-

---

3   Caroline Sawyer, "The Child Is Not a Person: Family Law and Other Legal Cultures," *Journal of Social Welfare and Family Law* 28, no. 1: 1-14.

er areas of law."[4] There are several assumptions in this citation that are worth pointing out. First, there is a glissade between being a social actor and being a legal personality. It is as if Sawyer cannot conceive of a social actor that interrupts the law, suspends it, disrupts it, or refuses it. If this were the case, then a host of revolutionary figures would be excluded from being conceptualized as viable social actors. Outlaws have no standing within the law and yet can function as important social actors (both in the sense of terrorists and as revolutionaries). Second, there is the assumption that personhood will solve or at least mitigate issues related to the fragilities and risks of childhood. Yet it seems clear that the extension of rights to other adult minorities who are equally at risk for violence and abuse has not always been an effective strategy (this is not even to mention the rather insufficient social, economic, and political results of international human rights).

There are two extremes embedded within this legal framework. The first concerns the child as abjected (abandoned) and the second concerns the child as object (of legal concern and state investment). Between the two is the more ambiguous status of the child as potentially a person or potentially a someone who could wear a mark of personhood. Whereas in the first case, this potentiality is subjected to the animal life of the child (de-personalization), in the second case, it is continually actualized through learning (personalization). Stated differently this potentiality can be equally actualized and not actualized. It can both lead to personalization or animalization. The child—within the legal paradigm of the family— rests precariously between these two positions.

---

4   Ibid., 2.

The dialectics of personalization and animalization suggest that personhood is an aporia that always results in the exclusion/sacrifice of something or someone. Stated differently the person always affects a separation between either (a) the individual subject and its pre-individual body (marked as animal) or (b) the social subject and its other (marked as racially or ethnically inferior). Inscriptions of personhood through law do not fill the gap between the public mask and private face which wears it so much as produce ever more displacements of the excess or surplus that lies at the exterior edge of the person. As such, merely arguing for the extension of personhood to those who have been traditionally excluded will not solve the central problem at hand. And this matters, especially for children who are precariously on the cusp of personhood.

But what is the alternative? In conclusion, I would like to suggest an *impersonal* education, one which lets idle the infernal dialectic of personalization and animalization. Another name for the impersonal is the common. The common is neither private nor public, neither internal nor external, neither personal nor animal. It is an indistinguishing threshold that suspends and renders inoperative these binaries that define not only the political landscape but also the educational. Impersonalization is the gesture of "anyone at all."[5] Anyone at all can attend this school. Anyone at all can be educated. Anyone at all can teach.

Anyone at all is the fundamental gesture of an education in common. There are four fundamental features of this gesture. First, the impersonal anyone interrupts the taken-for-granted logic underlying the constitution of the liberal subject. The

5   Esposito, *Third Person*, 125.

liberal subject is the person who *owns* his or her personhood as property (credentials, rights, privileges, qualitative and quantitative values). This property immunizes the liberal subject against any contamination from the outside (by granting them privileges, access, and recognition). An impersonal education would therefore have to shift paradigms from education as personal consumption and personal property (one buys and owns what one learns as cultural capital) to a fundamentally different paradigm. The impersonal anyone at all *owns nothing*, is *radically poor*, and is exposed to contamination. Second, if the liberal subject is granted mastery of and choice over his or her personal fate through the rights and privileges of personhood, then the impersonal anyone at all gives up mastery, embracing the contingencies of being-in-common, and finds in such exposure a new form-of-life.

Third, the liberal subject insists on personal rights, freedoms, and liberties, and his or her political actions are safeguards against invasion (by the state, by the immigrant, by the poor). As opposed to the reduction of the political to personal security, the collective character of engagement determines the character of the impersonal. The 99% is important in this respect for it indicates a new post-identity politics that is anonymous, impersonal, and thus radically common. The 99% is anyone at all. A common education is an education for and by the 99%.

Instead of an education, which attempts to divide the child against this impersonal life, can we not think of an education that would *celebrate* and *enrich* it? Can we not think of an education that sees the impersonal as a promise rather than a problem? My answer is an absolute YES. Indeed, anyone at all can imagine such an education.

CHAPTER 4

"To Be Less Than You Are": A Subject of Subtraction

In this paper, I want to briefly sketch out four possible ethical injunctions underlying any educational project concerning the question of the self—whether it be the question of self-actualization, self-acceptance, or self-cultivation.[1] It is my contention that the first three injunctions can be criticized for one or another type of determinism and developmentalism. These two are linked together in the sense that they both presuppose that function precedes form, determining in advance how something will grow, mature, or change. Perhaps we can state this simply as essence before existence. And while certain forms of determinism and developmentalism might be useful in educational settings, they also pose problems. Determinism has been criticized for promoting racism, sexism, and classism

---

[1]   This paper was delivered at the European Educational Research Association Conference, University College of Dublin, Ireland, 2016.

while developmentalism has been criticized by social psychology as being overly reductive and restrictive. In response to these worries, I propose a fourth formulation, which I align with a potentialist position against any form of determinism or developmentalism.

"Become what you are"

This injunction can be found in the Greek ideal of *paideia* wherein education is for those who are free and only in need of special skills and knowledge necessary to further develop this freedom.[2] Beginning with Plato's *Meno*, we see that education concerns the drawing out of what is always already existing within a student. In this dialogue, Plato demonstrates that an anonymous slave knows basic geometry although he has never actually been taught geometry by a teacher. Speaking through the character of Socrates, Plato states "the truth about reality is always in our soul."[3] According to Plato, the slave is able to produce geometric proofs because such knowledge lies within oneself. Learning on this reading is thus "recollection" of that which is dormant in the soul.[4] Indeed, the Latin word *educare* means to draw out that which lies inside, thus harkening back to a Platonic sense of making manifest and exterior that which is latent and interior. The consequence of this basic model is that we cannot really learn anything new. The teacher

---

2   Werner Jaeger, *Paideia: The Ideals of Greek Culture*, trans. G. Highet (New York: Oxford University Press, 1944).

3   Plato, *Five Dialogues: Euthyphro, Apology, Crito, Meno, Phaedo*, trans. G.M.A. Grube (Indianapolis: Hackett Publishing Company, 2002), 78.

4   Ibid.

can merely help facilitate the process of leading outward that which the student always already knows.

This theme can also be found in Plato's description of the function of education in his ideal republic. Here, Plato argues "each of the other citizens is to be directed to what he is naturally suited for, so that, doing the one work that is his own, he will become not many but one, and the whole city will itself be naturally one not many."[5] Good education produces good natures, and good natures are useful for preserving the social order of a just city-state. In the famous myth of the metals, Plato makes clear that each citizen is born with a special soul that predetermines how an individual will ideally fit within the social order. There is a strict division of labor here between craftspeople, guardians, and philosopher kings according to what nature has given them (what they are "naturally suited for"). Through educational trials, the soul of the individual will emerge, determining a set educational track that leads to a predetermined end point. The internal harmony of the soul will thus mirror the external harmony of the naturally ordered city-state, producing a reflective effect wherein inside and outside, self and other, private and public correspond without excess or surplus. "Become what you are" is thus an educational injunction to self-actualize that which is latent inside yourself.

The dangers of determinism are readily apparent in these various parables and or myths as one is reducible to what one always already is, justifying a highly stratified and static notion of self and community. Likewise, the specific educational tracks offered by Plato for the various kinds of citizenry sug-

---

5   Plato, *Republic*, trans. G. M. A. Grube (Indianapolis: Hackett Publishing Company, Inc., 1992), 98-99.

gest an equally static notion of development.

"Be what you are"

In this version, one is what one actually is without remainder. One is merely one's observable actions. One is what
one does. One's actions are the full extent of one's potentiality for being, resulting in educational behaviorism. While we
need not worry about the pitfalls of developmentalism, this
maxim results in a nihilistic vision of absolute determinism
under the guise of total self-acceptance. You simply are what
you are, and education can be nothing more than the celebration of this state of being. Interestingly, we can think of Gert
Biesta's recent criticism of constructivism in this light.[6] For Biesta, constructivism can only amount to a celebration of who
a student always already is through the facilitation of learning
experiences geared toward the student's existing interests and
desires. The message in these progressive classrooms is simply:
"Who you are is OK. Be yourself." Such self-acceptance, while
apparently liberatory, reveals itself not only to be determinist
in the extreme but also nihilistic for there is nothing beyond
the horizon of one's own self-absorbed life.

"Be what you become"

On this view, one is not held to any particular state of being, rather one gives in to the flow of experience without end.
"Be what you become" is an educational injunction endors-
ing radical self-creation. There is nothing here but the endless becoming different from what one was. This is infinitely

---

6   Gert Biesta, *The Beautiful Risk of Education* (New York: Routledge, 2014).

open-ended, process oriented, and radically pluralistic. When becoming is privileged, education rejects all determinism and developmentalism, and as such offers unlimited freedom from such obstacles.[7] Yet, I would suggest that this freedom is determined in the last instance by the very logic of neoliberal hubris which posits a kind of infinite productivity without restrictions. As such, there is also a hidden developmentalism at work with this position, for capitalism thrives through the perpetual development of profits. Without endlessly becoming-different, capitalism would cease to hold its power; it would cease to be able to continually adapt, mutate, and flow into all regions of life. In education, perhaps we see this position most esteemed in discourses of ludic, postmodern play, often attributed to Deleuze (among others). In such classrooms, self-creation and self-overcoming are seen as forms of educational freedom to invent and experiment with affective intensities, flows, and deterritorializing machines. Yet, as I am suggesting here, there is an underlying determinism and developmentalism involved with such phony Deleuzianism which compromises its otherwise radical claims.

"Be less than you are"

This is perhaps the most unusual of the four possible injunctions. Through his reflections on potentiality, Giorgio Agamben undoes any primacy given to determinism and developmentalism, both of which rest on the assumption that function and/or essence precede form and/or existence. Ag-

---

7   See Stephanie Springgay, *Body Knowledge and Curriculum* (New York: Peter Lang, 2008) for an example of this approach to education.

amben summarizes: "there is no essence, no historical or spiritual vocation, no biological destiny that humans must enact or realize."[8] Whatever humans are consists in "the simple fact of one's existence as possibility or potentiality."[9] The actuality of pre-existing structures/essences/souls is therefore suspended and rendered inoperative by that which exceeds any actualization of such structures/essences, leaving open the space and time for a life in potential—a life in excess of any developmentalism or determinism. For Agamben, every potentiality is also and equally an impotentiality, or an ability to *not* be this or that kind of subject.[10]

Thus far, this might sound a lot like "be what you become," yet there is an important difference. Whereas freedom in the first sense is precisely the freedom *to do or to be* something (through actualization), in the second sense, freedom is the freedom *to not do or not be* something (through an impotential suspension).

Indeed, being less than you are subtracts oneself from any developmental story of becoming just as much as it interrupts any post-foundationalist, post-modern, neoliberal becoming. This paradoxical formulation indicates that the self is never self-same, that the self is always capable of being less than what it is supposed to be. The limits of the self do not determine the scope of the self, for at the core of the self resides the smallest of differences, a quantum of impotential difference, an (in)ability

---

8   Giorgio Agamben, *The Coming Community*, trans. M. Hardt (Minneapolis: University of Minnesota Press, 1993), 43.

9   Ibid.

10   See the talks collected in Part II of this volume for a more comprehensive discussion of potentiality and impotentiality.

to be the self residing within the self itself. The self is *not* the self and yet also *not-not* the self. While "be what you become" results in a flow of mutations, a great "Yes!" to experience, "be less than what you are" offers up only a meager "I would prefer not to perform," which halts mutation in its tracks.

The strange freedom here is not a freedom in being what you are (touching your limit and residing there) or being what you become (overcoming all purported limits as merely false or temporary territorializations of self as perpetual motion machine) but rather a freedom in *receding from limits defining the self in terms of deterministic assumptions or developmental teleology.* This is freedom not to be who you are supposed to be or what you are supposed to become. This is freedom not to touch or overcome limits but rather limit the limitation of the limit by withdrawing into an (in)ability.

Features of self as not a self (or a self that is less than itself) could phenomenological be listed as follows. First, the self *as not* self is exhausted rather than productive. As I have argued elsewhere drawing on Deleuze, exhaustion is a state wherein one suffers one's potentiality without end.[11] To be tired, for Deleuze, is to actualize some sort of potentiality in relation to certain goals. Tiredness is a state familiar to anyone who tries to continually live up to his or her potentiality by making it operative. Indeed, to "be who you are" or to "become what you are" or "be what you become" all involve certain forms of being tired. They all demand evidence of oneself, and thus force potentiality to account for itself in the form of outputs

---

11   Tyson E. Lewis and Florelle D'Hoest, "Exhausting the Fatigue University: In Search of a Biopolitics of Research," *Ethics & Education* 10, no. 1 (2015): 49-60.

and standards of measure (here it does not matter so much if the standards are self-determined or not).

The self that is less than itself is also a distracted self. According to Paul North, distraction is precisely the name of a state of non-thinking wherein capacities are suspended and dispersed.[12] To be distracted means that one is not beholden to being-determining structures, categories, or processes or developmental trajectories.

The final dimension of the self as less than itself that I would like to highlight here is that such a self is de-personalized. Exhausted and distracted, this self is not in possession of itself. In my work, I have attempted to formalize a notion of the self that lacks the security and possessiveness of the liberal understanding of the self as in control of itself.[13] A de-personalized sense of self gives itself over to that which is less than itself. It is the self that is barely itself.

What this injunction means for education is rather obscure, but perhaps we can find an articulation in my theory of studying. The studier prefers not to be determined by any pre-existing forms of power (whether they be internal or external) and prefers not to abide by any developmental plan mapped in advance. Instead, the studier dwells in a state of impotential subtraction, never living up to his or her full potential, never actualizing his or her great promise, perpetually falling off track, constantly missing deadlines, and thus remaining in a zone of perplexity for those who demand self-actualization, self-affirmation, or self-creation as evidence that education is

---

12   Paul North, *The Problem of Distraction* (Stanford: Stanford University Press, 2011).

13   See Lewis, *On Study* and *Inoperative Learning*.

"working." The studier is not focused or attentive to one topic—doggedly pursuing it with single-minded focus—but rather roams through the library, distracted. And in this distracted state, is radically passionate about the (non) act of studying, about the impotentiality of thinking as such. There can be no end to this distraction, nor can the studier be measured in terms of his or her output or results. If there is freedom here, it is the smallest of freedoms: the freedom to be oneself *as not* oneself. Study is the minor space and time within education where the self can be less than itself (and thus risk the stupidity of exhaustion, distraction, and impersonality) without the threat of abandonment.

The "ethical" injunction to "be less than oneself" is therefore a paradoxical if not parodic injunction that does not specify a subject position (according to what can be determined or what can be developed). Whether given by a teacher to a student or by a student to him or herself, "to be less than oneself" is ultimately to *care for* the impotential remnant of one's potentiality and thus always leave open a space and time for an unpredicted form of educational life to emerge.

PART III

EDUCATIONAL POTENTIALISM

CHAPTER 5

ACTUALISM IN EDUCATIONAL PHILOSOPHY
AND PRACTICE:
A CRITIQUE

The working hypothesis of this paper is that educational philosophy has been predominantly defined by a privileging of actuality over and against potentiality.[1] My goal is to provide a sketch of this within educational philosophy and then draw forth several important implications for rethinking the starting point of education. Beginning with Plato's *Meno*, we see that education concerns the drawing out of what is already existing within the student.[2] Thus, we cannot really learn anything new. The teacher can merely make explicit the knowledge which the student always already knows. In this sense, what is actual (the implicit knowledge we carry with us)

---

1   This paper was first presented at the European Conference on Educational Research (ECER), Free University, Berlin (2011).

2   Plato, *Five Dialogues*.

determines in advance that which is possible.

The same is true for Aristotle. One can be educated to be an excellent person if one has *already* been habituated through training to enjoy that which is good and to be revolted by that which is bad. In his *Nicomachean Ethics*, Aristotle writes, "The character, then, must somehow be there already with a kinship to excellence, loving what is noble and hating what is base."[3] By the time the child receives ethical instruction in the virtues, he or she has been habituated to proper virtues and has learned to enjoy them but cannot yet appreciate the reasons for acting in accordance with virtue. To be truly virtuous, the child needs to be ethically reflective or gain a conscious understanding of who he or she is and why he or she is acting a certain way. Thus, formal instruction is needed to harmonize emotions with reason. Instruction enables someone who already has the preconditions for an excellent character to better understand what he or she should do and why. Instruction allows an individual to choose to be virtuous, and thus cultivate true practical wisdom or phronesis. Ethical education, on this view, presupposes the actuality of the very traits that it articulates in the form of a theory of excellence. Without proper habituation, as Aristotle warns, instruction would not be able to sway someone from finding pleasure in the wrong objects at the wrong times in the wrong ways.

This privileging of what is actual as the determining factor for education carries through much of educational philosophy and comes to take many forms. In critical sociology of schooling, for instance, there is the assumption that one can only

---

3   Aristotle, *The Complete Works of Aristotle*, trans. J. Barnes (Princeton: Princeton University Press, 1984), 1864.

learn what is determined in advance by one's position within the social relations of production.[4] And in progressivism, as Gert Biesta has recently pointed out, constructivism can never expose the student to anything outside of their existing world, interests, and desires, thus limiting what can be learned to that which has always already been learned.[5] In all cases, the inheritance of Plato is clear: learning concerns what is already there. It is a repetition of what is actually existing thrown into relief, brought to conscious thought, turned into a vocation, and so forth.

Yet there are dangers associated with the dominance of actualism in education. First, there is the danger of determinism. It is my contention that racism, sexism, and classism are always forms of actualism wherein the potential of the individual is reduced to their actual skin color or their biological sex. We see this in Rousseau's deterministic educational philosophy where one's biological sex offers the preconditions for what kind of education one receives.[6] Or we see this in the mental hygiene movement in the United States wherein racial traits determine in advance one's potentiality for this or that.[7] Or we can think of dominant stereotypes of the poor according to any number of deficit models (the poor are lazy and stupid and therefore deserve to be poor).

---

4   See Rancière's critique of Pierre Bourdieu in *The Philosopher and His Poor*, trans. A. Parker (Durham: Duke University Press, 2004).

5   See Biesta, *Beyond Learning*.

6   Jean-Jacques Rousseau, *Emile: Or on Education*, trans. Allan Bloom (New York: Basic Books, 1979).

7   Tyson E. Lewis, "Education and the Immunization Paradigm," *Studies in Philosophy and Education* 28, no. 6(2009): 485-498.

The second danger is developmentalism. When one starts from the point of what is actual, then such actuality is not negated but developed through learning to become manifest to itself (in Hegel's language, more determinant). In all the theories outlined above, education is the development of the seed into the tree or of the implicit into the explicit or the latent into the manifest. As Nietzsche once said, one must become what one already is. This is a kind of mantra for educational actualism where the actual is privileged over and above potentiality. The problem here is not so much discrimination (as with the first danger) but with the erasure of the contingency of existence. Instead of the potential to be otherwise than what is mapped out for one in advance, we have nothing less than a pure necessity: things must be such and such a way according to existing conditions (what is actual).

Determinism and developmentalism are captured in Plato's theory of the souls. Each is determined ahead of time and education is the development of said abilities toward socially desirable outcomes within the division of labor. Any class-based, racist, and sexist society is predicated on some version of determinism and/or developmentalism (work hard and you will progress, pull yourself up by your bootstraps, might makes right).

A critique of actualism thus opens up the space to think the beginning of educational practice free from the tyranny of the actual and returns us to the question of potentiality.

Agamben offers a new starting point, one that does not privilege actuality over and above potentiality. As he writes, "that which is not (*ta mē onta*) is stronger than that which is."[8]

---

8   Giorgio Agamben, *The Time That Remains: A Commentary on*

Education is always concerned with what can be actualized, and thus its enemy is precisely that which is not (the impotential dimension of potentiality that withdraws from actualization). We teach to measure what can be actualized; we teach in order for potentiality to pass seamlessly into actuality without remainder. *The* educational imperative is "actualize your potentiality," but what Agamben offers is something else, something much more peculiar: an impotential education.

When we privilege potentiality, we do not simply or easily flip the equation. Instead, what is produced is an actualization of that which the act of actualizing usually destroys: potentiality's impotential remnant, or potentiality's ability to not be. What then would it mean for impotentiality to pass into actuality without being destroyed or negated? Paradoxically, it would result in an actualization of that which prefers not to be actualized, a de-actualization. Such de-actualization cannot be measured, and as such, would not be of value in the frameworks of either developmentalism or determinism.

Educational life for potentiality against actuality is thus not a privation or a retreat into a state of doing nothing. It is rather a state of doing justice to the contingency that impotentiality opens up, the work that impotentiality does to dislodge the developmentalism and determinism infesting education. An impotential educational life is a life without measure, without positive location within the actually existing order of things. It is an educational life that is otherwise than that which is predetermined, predicted, and otherwise held captive by the actual. Take for instance the idea of class repro-

the Letter to the Romans, trans. P. Dailey (Stanford, Stanford University Press, 2005), 41.

duction. Actualism would insist that one must become what one already is through education: a member of the working class. Critical sociology confirms this repeatedly, highlighting the role of schooling in merely perpetuating class distinctions, as if there is no alternative. Yet, potentialism would highlight the opposite situation in which one prefers not to join the class of which one is a part. Instead, one would become a member of the working class *as not* a member of that class, inserting a remnant into the ordering of society according to class divisions. This would be an inoperative worker, or someone in exodus from the work that has been assigned to him or her. And this makes possible another way of being and doing "class" outside of mere economic reproduction.

Is there a name or place in which such impotential can be "actualized" (instead of merely being destroyed)? If so, it will be on the margins, in the back alleys, in the dark corners, or as Stefano Harney and Fred Moten state, in the "undercommons" where groups of studiers meet despite being tossed out of school, where those who were deemed "dropouts" or "idiots" or "at-risk" suddenly discover that although they prefer not to engage in learning, they are certainly open to the possibility of study as an impotential form of educational life.[9]

---

9   Harney and Moten, *Undercommons.*

CHAPTER 6

VITA ACTIVA AND THE INOPERATIVITY OF
EDUCATIONAL SUSPENSION

In celebration of the 50th anniversary of Hannah Arendt's essay "The Crisis in Education" and her classic text *The Human Condition, Teachers College Press* published a special issue on Arendt featuring an impressive array of scholars each arguing for Arendt's on-going relevance.[1] A key question highlighted in several essays in this collection concerns the following: What is the location of education in Arendt's description of *vita activa*? In her attempt to understand the human condition in terms of labor, work, and action, Arendt seems to leave out any analysis of education, and in turn, her analysis of education seems to exclude the key question of labor, work, and action.

There are perhaps three explanations for this paradox.

---

1   This paper was presented at the European Educational Research Association Conference, University College of Dublin, Ireland (2016).

First, Arendt's work is simply missing a key connection and thus lacks a critical, synthetic moment that would bring education into contact with the rest of her analysis of the *vita activa* defining the human condition. On this reading, Arendt would be at fault and her analysis would be philosophically incomplete or fragmented. This is perhaps the least generous of possible explanations and fails to keep in mind the numerous possible reconstructions of these relations developed throughout many of the essays in the *Teachers College Press* special issue. The second potential reading is that the answer to the paradox is found within her description of labor, work, and action. This seems to be the route taken by Chris Higgins, who suggests that through a close reading of Arendt, we can determine that education is in fact a peculiar type of action— an action that is poised between work and action, private and public.[2] In this sense, Higgins, as well as many of the other contributors to the special issue, follows the lead of Arendtian scholar Aaron Schutz, who argues that while schools are not publics, they could be considered "quasi-publics" where the work of education is to provide opportunities to engage in certain types of action.[3] While an ingenious reading of Arendt, this argument seems to miss what is most perplexing and challenging about Arendt's work: that she does not consider education to be a part of the *vita activa*.

But, there is a third possibility: education has no place in

2   Chris Higgins, *The Good Life of Teaching: An Ethics of Professional Practice* (London: Wiley-Blackwell, 2011).

3   Aaron Shutz, "Is Political Education an Oxymoron? Hannah Arendt's Resistance to Public Spaces in Schools," in *Philosophy of Education Yearbook, 2001* (Urbana-Champaign: University of Illinois Press, 2001), 330.

Arendt's *vita activa* because it is not labor, work, or activity. Arendt's exclusion of education from *On the Human Condition* is not a mere oversight. Through the rest of this essay, I will explore this third possibility. In particular I will argue that education is the *impotentiality* of labor, work, and activity, and is thus included through its exclusion in the *vita activa*.

Vita Activa: An Overview

Without being overly reductive, I would like to sketch out the three forms of life which Arendt describes in *The Human Condition*. I suggest as a useful organizational tool the following graph.

Means	Agent	End	Logic	Relation
Labor	Homo Laborans	Survival	Necessity	Worldless, Private
Work	Homo Faber	Durability	Utility	The Commons (Shared World)
Action	Bios Politicos	Freedom	Newness	Public (Presence of Others in a World)

For Arendt, humans are, on a base, biological level, "enslaved by necessity," and this slavery demands that we eat, sleep, reproduce, and maintain basic functions out of the pure necessity to survive.[4] What all these diverse activities share is

---

4   Hannah Arendt, *The Human Condition* (Chicago: University of Chicago Press, 1998), 83.

that they are all manifestations of labor which preserve our private sustenance. While essential for defining the *vita activa*, labor is only one component—and perhaps the most generic and least distinctive. When taken to an extreme, labor overrides the other dimensions of the *vita activa* producing a world of meaningless ritual and endless cycles of consumption and repetition.

Between humans and nature, work erects and sustains the commonwealth which in turn makes the world possible. Arendt writes that work "guarantees the permanence and durability without which a world would not be possible at all."[5] Beyond incessant consumption and reproduction, work reifies deeds, facts, events, patterns, objects that are remembered and transformed into objective things—into sayings, stories, books, sculptures, records, documents, and monuments. Here, Arendt emphasizes the importance of remembering, reciting, and caring for the products of work. The problem with the dominance of work in the active life is when "usefulness and utility are established as the ultimate standards for life and the world of men" results in growing meaninglessness of life, a pure instrumentality or a "public without politics."[6] Thus like labor, work, when taken to an extreme, overshadows the complexity of the *vita activa* resulting in a fundamental impoverishment of the human condition.

With speech and action, individuals distinguish themselves from each other beyond mere necessity or utility through their deeds in the world. To act is to bring something new into the world, to take a risk and to begin to set something

5   Ibid., 94.

6   Ibid., 160.

in motion that cannot necessarily be predicted or anticipated in terms of its specific outcomes. Once something new is introduced into the world (the deed that results from a specific action), the very fact of our plurality makes the results of any one action unknown and immeasurable according to the existing world. It is through action and action alone that change is introduced into the world and individual bios, which is composed of deeds, makes itself known.

So, the question becomes: Where does education belong in this list? Is it work, labor, or action? More often than not, it would seem that education is thought under the sign of work, labor, and action. For instance:

1) Labor: Education as labor sees the educational process as mere extension of survival and thus reduces learning to the reproduction of labor power. Here we can think of neo-liberal educational reform which sees teachers as employees and students as consumers or as paid laborers receiving an actual salary for attendance and performance.[7] In this scenario, teaching is a technical job, and learning is mere consumption. Teaching as labor reduces education to learning for passing tests—a kind of brute educational survival for both the teacher—whose job is at stake if test scores are not improved—and the student—whose future employability is being evaluated.

2) Work: Education viewed as work insists on the priority of utility in the production of things in the world. More than simply test oriented education, it is product-orient-

7   Gregg Toppo, "Good Grades Pay Off Literally," *USA Today*, 27 January 2008.

ed education. Here we might think of higher education where research in labs must produce objects and information or produce discoveries or else research projects are not funded. This often results in the shrinking of humanities departments because they have no measurable utility in the fast-paced race for research and development.

3) Action: Scholars such as Chris Higgins suggest that education is a quasi-action and schools are quasi-publics. Citing Arendt, Higgins argues that deeds resulting from the surprising appearance of action have three features: theatricality, singularity, and unpredictability. They arise not out of habit or custom but out of the capacity Arendt calls "natality." Natality represents a clearing or opening in the world for a new subjectivization to emerge, or what Higgins calls the "self-disclosure" of the newcomer. Thus, if labor enables us to survive, work enables us to create a durable world of things, then action enables us to appear as ourselves in relation to others in the space of the public world. Education is a medial space between public and private, between work and action and thus conserves the world from the appearance of the new and the new against the old-ness of the world. According to Higgins, "the school erects only three walls around its students, opening the fourth, as the theatre does, to the public world."[8]   In this space, students, like political actors, try out various masks as an intrinsic part of "being yourself"

---

8   Chris Higgins, "Human Conditions for Teaching: The Place of Pedagogy in Arendt's *Vita Activa*," *Teachers College Record* 112, no. 2 (2010): 431.

in a "dramatic role"[9] that sparks natality, enlivens its potentiality for newness. In sum, "If all action is theatrical and involves elements of representation of, and response to, the scripts of culture, the classroom space seems best described as a full dress rehearsal."[10] In this dress rehearsal, the teacher as actor/director helps students "dramaturgically with questions of how to interpret and find themselves in the cultural, curricular material" and the classroom becomes a stage "where students can step forth in the presence of others and enact themselves, flashing something of their personhood that upends our expectations, cuts against the grain of conventions, and surprises even themselves."[11] But if education is a peculiar type of action (a "dress rehearsal"), this fragile distinction ultimately collapses when, later in the essay, he cites Toporkov who suggests that "the dress rehearsal is in a certain sense as real as it gets."[12] In an attempt to sidestep the issue of "developmentalism" or "pedagogic baptism,"[13] Higgins folds education into action thus losing the distinction that Arendt desires to maintain.

Simply subsuming education under work, labor, or action does not seem to hold true to Arendt's unique problematic.

9   Ibid., 433.

10   Ibid., 435.

11   Ibid., 436.

12   Ibid., 435.

13   Jan Masschelein and Maarten Simons, "Schools as Architectures for Newcomers and Strangers: The Perfect School as Public School?" *Teachers College Press* 112, no. 2 (2010): 531-555.

What if we took a radically different approach—one which does not see Arendt's exclusion of education from the *vita activa* as an oversight but as an insight? Here I want to turn to Arendt's essay "The Crisis in Education" for some possible alternatives.

From this essay, I want to draw three conclusions:

1) Education, like action, concerns language and speech, but it "can play no part in politics."[14]

2) Education, like work, concerns the construction and stability of the world, and thus concerns remembering and reciting, but it cannot be a pure instrumentality or utility which fetishizes or reifies the world.

3) Education, like labor, is fundamentally necessary for human flourishing, yet it is linked to the human world rather than pure biological existence.

Thus, education shares elements of labor, work, and action but is not reducible to any one of these three conditions. It is a space for feeling the potentiality for labor, work, and politics without being labor, work, or action. At the same time, education is not simply an introduction to or preparation for the *vita activa* either. So, what is the location of education within the human condition? Education is the experience of a potentiality that contains within itself aspects of labor, work, and action released from their specific agents, differing logics, and unique ends—opening them up to free use. If education

---

14   Hannah Arendt, *Between Past and Future: Eight Exercises in Political Thought* (New York: Penguin Books, 1968), 177.

pushes students to actualize their potentialities for labor, work, and action, it equally withdraws from such actualization in order to allow students to feel their potentialities as such. It does so through suspending—ever so slightly—the actualization of labor, work, and action so that they do not, in the end, equal themselves, but rather subtract themselves from themselves (labor *as not* labor, work *as not* work, action *as not* action).

According to Agamben, potentiality is the ability to conserve the ability to be *and* not to be, do *and* not do, within itself as a kind of impossible synthesis. By conserving itself, potential remains impotential. Thus, all theories of potentiality (capability to do) must also and equally be theories of impotentiality (capability not to do). To be "in potential" means "*to be in relation to one's own incapacity*."[15] For Arendt, education allows us to "conserve world against the new and the new against the world"[16] without destroying either. To conserve natality, we must conserve natality as both a potentiality and an impotentiality for this and that form of labor, work, and action, otherwise education collapses into labor or work. In addition, because education is not a form of action, it cannot be a form of self-disclosure and thus subjectivization, as Higgins argues. Education is not so much a form of subjectification as it is a de-subjectification or suspension between being and becoming this or that subject in the moment of conserving natality's fundamental impotentiality. For this very reason, students are not responsible for what is produced in the classroom in the same way an actor is responsible for his

---

15   Giorgio Agamben, *Potentialities*, trans. D. Heller-Roazen (Stanford: Stanford University Press, 1999), 182.

16   Arendt, *Past and Future*, 192.

or her deeds.

In sum, education is included through its exclusion in the *vita activa*. In other words, education is the *inoperativity* of labor, work, and action in a moment of suspended animation and of withdrawing from measurable ends. Education conserves when it enables us to experience our impotentiality through temporarily letting idle the necessity of labor, the utility of work, or the deeds of action. Another name for such an education is study.

CHAPTER 7

Inoperative Teacher Education

To invent a new language of teaching beyond learnification, Gert Biesta returns to the essential, ontological question of teaching in general, but also of teacher education more specifically.[1] Inspired by Aristotle, he proposes that teaching could be conceptualized as either *poiesis* (making action) or *praxis* (doing action). *Poiesis* is the creation of something through technical skill. *Praxis* on the other hand does not concern itself with creating something so much as with promoting *eudemonia* or human flourishing. For Biesta, teaching cannot be thought of as a making of a product. Certainly, teachers make material things such as curricular materials, and extending the idea of making beyond the realm of material things, we also might want to produce effective citizens or effective thinkers. Key here is the connection that Biesta draws between *poie-*

---

1   This paper was delivered at the European Educational Research Association Conference, University College of Dublin, Ireland (2016).

sis and "effectiveness."[2] When effectiveness is extended to the social realm or to educational relations between teachers and students, education becomes reduced to a version of learning, teaching to an instrumental practice that meets predetermined goals through predetermined, effective techniques.

Considering these dangers, Biesta turns toward teaching as a *praxis. Praxis* affords him the opportunity to move beyond teaching as a merely technical endeavor concerned with the relationship between inputs and outputs. If teaching is a hermeneutical, communicative, and political act, then what is needed in teacher education courses is not competencies so much as virtues of judgment. Teacher education beyond learnification cultivates virtuous practice, and the ideal of the teacher as a *phronimos*. Biesta summarizes as follows, "Educational judgments are, after all, judgments about what needs to be done, not with the aim to produce something in the technical sense but with the aim to bring about what is considered to be educationally desirable."[3] Teacher education should concern itself less with acquisition of technical skills and knowledge and more with existential, political, and ethical questions concerning the purposes of teaching that are essential components in any act of judgment. Teachers make a multitude of judgments every day in their practices, and such judging is hermeneutical in nature. Thus, the good life of teaching is found in the moments when teachers *risk something of themselves* in their judgments.

Here, Biesta is to be given credit for his on-going polemic against the reduction of education to learning and teaching to

2   Biesta, *The Beautiful Risk of Education*, 113.

3   Ibid., 134.

facilitation. As I have argued elsewhere, learnification is the educational logic of late capitalism, and as such, a communist struggle in education is a fight against the transposition of financial logics into an educational sphere (not unlike Althusser's struggle to keep idealism out of materialist philosophy).[4] Yet what I would like to do is problematize Biesta's turn toward teaching as a *praxis*. I agree in full that we cannot simply state that teaching is about making action, but his wholesale emphasis on teaching as a doing action does not actually solve the central problem: the problem of aligning teaching with effectiveness.

Teachers, for Biesta, have an ethical duty to actualize wise judgments for their students; teachers must be effective ethical role models. But as the concluding chapter of Biesta's book reveals, a virtues approach to teacher education does not escape the lure of effectiveness so much as substitute one form of effectiveness for another. Teacher education should aim to produce "virtuosity" through the study of "wise educational judgments."[5] Instead of competencies we have virtues, instead of empirical tests we have hermeneutical judgments. In both cases, what is emphasized is the *operativity of teaching*. Biesta clearly argues that the teacher is someone who "has to bring something to the educational situation that was not there already" and that this something has to come from the radical outside.[6] They have to make virtuous judgment, wisdom, and so forth appear; they have to make operative their capacity for judgment by actualizing this capacity by bringing something

4   Lewis, *Inoperative Learning.*

5   Biesta, *Beautiful Risk of Education,* 136.

6   Ibid., 6.

to the educational situation that is not already there.

Again, I see much merit in Biesta's analysis, but I do have one worry. According to the recent work of Agamben, the philosophical history of the virtues links them directly to questions of modern conceptualizations of effectivity. Although providing the spacing/separation necessary for us to think the aporia of potentiality as such, Aristotle repeatedly emphasizes the supremacy of the act over potentiality and habit. Agamben observes the following, "In this sense the potential-act distinction in Aristotle is certainly ontological (*dynamis* and *energeia* are 'two ways in which being is said'): nevertheless, precisely because it introduces a division into being and afterward affirms the primacy of *energia* over *dynamis*, it implicitly contains an orientation of being toward operativity."[7] Aristotle in other words orients being toward what is done or realized by an agent. This is a decisive step that opens up the door for a sea change in Western metaphysics from being as what exists to *being as what is done* through a *praxis*.

From the perspective of *praxis*, potentiality becomes an increasing problem that must be solved so that potentiality can be put to work and fulfill a *telos*. To overcome the inoperativity of habit (its latent potentiality not to actualize itself), Aristotle develops a theory of the virtues. As Agamben writes, the virtues are precisely an attempt to "render governable"[8] the potentiality-not-to-act. They ensure the passage from potentiality to acting at the right time, in the right way, with the right feeling, toward the right things and people. Virtue

---

7   Giorgio Agamben, *Opus Dei: An Archeology of Duty*, trans. A. Kotsko (Stanford: University of Stanford Press, 2013), 53.

8   Ibid., 96.

is the becoming operative of potentiality in relation to a particular *ethos* or set of customs. The virtues are precisely a form of governmentality of the self by the self to ensure that one's capabilities pass into actuality and thus made operative. They make the potentiality of our capabilities operative and thus *effective*. Christian scholastics from Cicero to Aquinas to Ambrose develop this latent strand of Aristotle's ontology until potentiality is, as Agamben argues, "bracketed" completely.[9] Being is found in one's doing. Or rather being is doing *without remainder*. "The good (virtuous)," summarizes Agamben, "is such because it acts well and acts well because it is good (virtuous)."[10] The categorical distinction in classical ontology between potentiality and act, being and *praxis* are rendered indistinct, collapsing into one another until being is only an acting. And during the course of this transformation, *dynamis* is replaced with effectiveness. Here lies the roots of modern ontologies of *praxis* in which potentiality (as the capability to do and not to) is only included as an exclusion.

Although Biesta is keen on linking *poiesis* with effectiveness (and thus separating himself from this terminology), he misses how a certain form of effectiveness is intrinsic to his description of *praxis* as well. While in one sense he argues for a redefinition of learning as risky exposure to that which is beyond one's personal subjectivity and for a redefinition of teaching as a vulnerable and precarious practice beyond measure, in another sense, his turn toward virtuosity still remains firmly within the very same lineage of effectiveness that goes back to Aristotle's privileging of acting over potentiality. For

9   Ibid., 99.

10   Ibid., 100.

Biesta, to be a teacher means that one must be virtuous, and this virtuosity must be effectuated, must be actualized in the form of wise judgments. Biesta argues that teacher education should be oriented around virtues instead of competencies. These virtues, as Aristotle would argue, only develop through practice. He suggests that a major component of teacher education should be "that we develop our virtuosity for wise educational judgment only by *practicing* judgment, that is, by being engaged in making such judgment in the widest range of educational situations possible."[11] In the field, preservice teachers can observe "the ways in which teachers make embodied and situated wise educational judgments."[12] As such, observing the virtuosity of others emphasizes what teachers do. Who teachers are is observed in how they judge. In this subtle way *praxis* is decisively circular in nature: the teacher's being defines the practice but only in-so-far as the practice defines such being. Work and being collapse into one another.

While the difference between virtues and competencies, value judgments and technical application, learning from and being taught by are interesting distinctions that bear educationally relevant fruit, what is most important in my account is how the same ontology of effectiveness underlies each of these in subtle ways missed by Biesta. The virtues, as portrayed in Agamben's genealogy, are an apparatus of government: they ensure the actualization of wise judgment. Simply stated, virtuosity is not simply potential or actual but rather that which is manifest only through its operation (through judgment). To be a teacher is to coincide with the effectiveness of one's

---

11   Ibid., 135.

12   Ibid., 136.

potentiality to judge wisely.

What is at stake here is confronting teacher education with the aporia of potentiality, of the remainder that resists becoming operative, that exceeds praxis, that interrupts any measure of what it means to be a "good" or effective teacher. Teacher education, on this view, would not be about *learning* to actualize wise judgments but about something else entirely and the teacher educator would be something more and less than a virtuous role model.

But if teacher education is not a form of making action or doing action, then what is it? What is teacher education beyond any imperative to be effective or to be wise? Here we need to take very seriously the question of the gesture. Drawing on Aristotle, Agamben argues that gestures are special in that they are neither a form of *praxis* nor *poiesis*. Whereas action aims at an end internal to itself and production aims at an end external to itself, gesture removes means from an end (internal or external). In sum, Agamben argues that the gesture is "neither production nor enactment but undertaking and supporting."[13] Certain aesthetic forms display the pure mediality of gestures.

One such aesthetic form is mime. In mime, gestures "directed toward the most familiar ends are displayed as such, and therefore, held in suspense [...] thus in gesture, there is the sphere not of an end in itself, but of a kind of mediation that is pure and devoid of any end that is effectively communicated to people."[14]   For instance, miming the gesture of drinking water means that the gesture of picking up the glass, raising it

---

13   Giorgio Agamben, *Infancy and History: On the Destruction of Experience*, trans. L. Heron (London: Verso, 2007), 154.

14   Ibid., 155.

to one's mouth, and tilting back the head to receive the liquid is performed, yet the utilitarian end of the gesture (satisfying thirst) is deactivated. What remains is only the use of the gesture in its nudity and immediacy. The inoperativity of the gesture, according to Agamben's reading, then "allows the very potentiality that has manifested itself in the act to appear."[15] What is rendered inoperative through mime is not potentiality, but only its ends. The result is an action that achieves nothing beyond making appear its own potentiality for appearing, its gesture.

What the teacher educator as mime exhibits is not *how* to teach or *what* to teach but that we *all have the capability* to teach and not to teach. Once teacherly gestures are released from their ends (and thus deactivated from the imperative to make effective or make wise), they can be exhibited as such, without specific destination or utilization. Yet what I am arguing here is that the teacher educator does not have to bring something new into the educational situation; rather, the teacher educator exhibits the gesture of bringing something new, exhibits the gestural support for doing or making without doing or making anything. As such, the teacher educator's gestures are in potential in that they are in use but only insofar as their utilization for any specific ends is left idle.

The nude gestures of the teacher educator assist with studying rather than learning. When the gestures appear, they can be contemplated. What is virtue? What does it mean to be a virtuous teacher? Is that virtue? Could it be different? These are the questions that arise from an inoperative teacher edu-

---

15   Giorgio Agamben, *Nudities*, trans. A. Kotsko (Stanford: Stanford University Press, 2009), 102.

cation where virtue is not actualized/made effective so much as potentiated through gesture. Actualizing virtues, observing them, and thus learning by example are all suspended. What remains is a community of studiers who are confronted with gestures released from their purported ends. Whereas for Biesta, teacher educators must make virtue appear through their practice of judgment, here I am suggesting that teacher education take a weaker and more ambiguous path: the path of potentiality, making appear the gestures supporting virtuous (wise) ends without themselves exhibiting such wisdom. If teacher education is a praxis as Biesta argues, it is an *inoperative praxis* that deactivates teaching (as a model) so that the gestures of the teacher can appear (now open to anyone).

Perhaps we can end at this point with a hope: that students will enter our teacher education courses with high expectations to learn how to be the best teachers (virtuous or otherwise), and they will leave with a queer smile on their faces that seems to say: "I am not sure I learned anything in that class that will help me become a teacher or help me define virtuous teaching, but it certainly did cause me to think."

CHAPTER 8

Beyond the Law of Learning: From Self-Slander to Self-Potentialization in the Studious Classroom

I want to start with a common occurrence in education.[1] We have all, I am sure, experienced a student coming up to us and saying something like the following: "I'm really sorry, but I didn't finish the homework; sometimes I'm just so stupid." A variant of this might be: "I don't get it; I can't do math." From a psychological point of view, such phrases might speak to the onset of depression. Indeed, the psychotherapist and author of the best-selling book *When Kids Call the Shots*, Sean Grover, argues that this kind of self-deprecation is a key manifestation of low self-esteem that should be actively combatted with psychotherapy, creativity, and educational opportunities (learning new skills, for instance). Such an interpretation assumes that

---

1   This presentation was part of the Lecture Series in New Social Theory and Education at Adelphi University, NYC, 2013.

the student is *revealing* something truthful about his or her condition and that the concurrent judgment—"I'm stupid"— is something the student genuinely *believes* to be the case. There is thus an assumed correlation between the statement and the actual state of affairs. Certainly, such an interpretation might be the case in certain instances and the need for psychotherapy and or educational modifications might very well be called for to provide relief, but this need not hold universally. Instead of immediately pathologizing students when they say, "I'm not a math person," I would like to pause and consider an alternative interpretation. What I am concerned with here is thinking through such statements as forms of *self-slander* or, as tactics to subvert the law—the law of learning. In this sense, I want to read the self-slander of students as a *political* act rather than *psychological* symptom. To do so, I will turn to Agamben's analysis of self-slander in his essay titled "K." I will then suggest that while self-slander does offer up one potential response to the law, it is ultimately an ineffective one. For students, it does not suspend the law so much as reinscribe it. Instead, I will suggest an alternative activity that results in self-potentialization: study.

Self-Slander

Agamben's work is useful to focus on the paradoxical sense of agency that arises through acts of self-slander, especially for those who are otherwise denied agency under the law. Indeed, self-slander is a tactic that actually opens up a paradox at the heart of the law as such in order to exploit this paradox. Simply put, self-slander happens when the self is innocent of the charges which the self accuses the self of. As such, the self is

guilty of the crime of self-slander insofar as the self is innocent. This paradoxical state of being wherein guilt and innocence correspond interrupts the smooth functioning of accusation and judicial decision making which rests on being able
to establish distinctions.

Perhaps the most insightful commentary on self-slander
can be found in the work of Franz Kafka. Indeed, Agamben
has pointed out that the initial K. in the name Josef K. from
the novel *The Trial* does not simply stand for "Kafka" but
rather for slanderer. In ancient Roman law, the individual accused of slander was marked on the forehead with the letter K,
which stood for *kalumniator* or slanderer. If this is indeed the
case, then Agamben is correct in locating at the heart of Kafka's enigmatic work the question of slander, and in particular,
self-slander. This strategy enables Agamben to pinpoint the
ultimate accuser of the *Trial*: Josef K. himself! Summarizing,
Agamben argues, "Even though K. actually knows right from
the start that there is no way to be completely certain that he
has been accused by the court [...], and that at any rate his
condition of being 'under arrest' does not imply any change in
his life, he still tries in every conceivable way to penetrate the
court buildings [...] and to instigate a trial that the judges do
not seem to have any intention of initiating."[2] Josef K. presents
himself to court when it is not in session, and he even suggests
in a conversation with Miss Bürstner that she falsely accuse
him of assault. In both cases, and many others to boot, Josef
K. willingly, if not eagerly, engages in acts of slander against
his own innocence.

But why does Josef K. work so hard to inscribe himself

---

2   Agamben, *Nudities*, 21.

in the law? Here we have to remember the peculiar paradox of self-slander: that it seems to render the very foundation of the law to pass judgments inoperative. On this reading, K.'s actions become attempts to deactivate the law by highlighting its internal paradox. For Agamben, "Self-slander is part of Kafka's strategy in his incessant struggle with the law. In the first place, it calls guilt into question or, more precisely, the principle according to which there is no punishment without guilt."[3] How can one be guilty of self-slander if one is only a slanderer in so far as the self is innocent of the accusation? Furthermore, how can one separate the accusation of a crime from the crime itself? Agamben concludes, "One understands, then, the subtlety of self-slander as a strategy that seeks to deactivate and render inoperative the accusation, the indictment that the law addresses toward Being."[4] Guilt becomes indistinct from innocence and accusation becomes indistinct from the crime. In this way, the foundational principles of the law show themselves to be uncertain or indeterminate. A decision cannot be reached, and the legal apparatus becomes inoperative. What appears to be a purely passive acquiescence to the law, in reality, inaugurates a prolonged deferral of the law's power to condemn K.

Yet, for Agamben, self-slander as a political gesture to interrupt the smooth functioning of the law ultimately backfires. Concerning Kafka, Agamben writes, "Kafka is indeed completely aware of the insufficiency of this strategy, since the response of the law is to transform the indictment [self-slander] itself into a crime, and to turn self-slander into its foun-

3   Ibid., 23.

4   Ibid., 24.

dation."[5] The law merely absorbs the slander into itself. While slander reveals how the law rests on shaky grounds, the law is nevertheless able to argue that it is necessary to judge which statements are, in the end, groundless slander and which are merited. The law wants to therefore assert that it is above the baseness of slander all the while transforming the paradox of slander into a machine for reproducing the power of the law.

Kafka's work concerns the law, and Agamben's interpretation focuses on the juridical implications of Kafka's fiction. But we can see how a similar drama might play out in classrooms. Returning to my opening example, we could interpret the statement "I can't do math" as a kind of self-slander that is not merely a reflection of a student's actual abilities but is instead an act of self-slander before the law. The law here is the law of learning. By "law of learning" I am referring to Agamben's rather broad definition of law: "we mean by this term [law] the entire text of tradition in its regulative form."[6] In other words, law refers to explicit and implicit forms of regulation, control, and capture that constitute the lived facticity of our experience in the world.

While some might argue that law (as a regulative set of ideas, practices, and norms) is a purely historical and cultural concept, learning is a naturally occurring human capacity. Yet this assumption misses how learning itself is also historically and culturally determined. Indeed, we cannot understand the nature of learning today outside of what some have called

---

5   Ibid., 24-25.

6   Giorgio Agamben, *Homo Sacer: Sovereign Power and Bare Life*, trans. D. Heller-Roazen (Stanford: Stanford University Press, 1998), 51.

the "learning society."[7] Within a flexible, knowledge-driven, neoliberal economy, laborers must become "life-long learners" constantly optimizing their labor through reskilling. Thus, the dominance of discourses and practices of learning dovetails with certain economic needs to the point where learning and laboring become largely indistinct (or at least mutually reinforcing). Likewise, Gert Biesta argues that the learning prevalent today transforms educational relations into economic transactions in which "the teacher, the educator, or the educational institution is seen as the provider, that is, the one who is there to meet the needs of the learner, and where education itself becomes a commodity—a 'thing'—to be provided or delivered by the teacher or educational institution and to be consumed by the learner."[8] On both accounts, learning is not simply naturally given, but is a historically specific manifestation of education according to certain economic logics.

I would add to this economic reading of learning a juridical dimension. Learning within the learning society follows its own internal law, or regulative ideals.[9] Whether one is referring to authentic learning, deep learning, situated learning, or standardized learning, there is a consistent law to be followed: (a) there is an intention to learn which (b) informs the selection and planning of experiences through which (c) growth, development, or progress are measured. This learning process is verified by assessment (formal and informal). The

---

7   Jan Masschelein, Maaren Simons, Ulrich Bröckling, and Ludwig Pongratz (eds.), *The Learning Society From the Perspective of Governmentality* (London: Wiley-Blackwell, 2007).

8   Biesta, *Beyond Learning*, 20.

9   Lewis, *Inoperative Learning*.

law of learning thus includes an ultimate judgment concerning what has been learned, how well it has been learned, and what can be expected in the future. The law ensures that there is a connection (of some kind) between inputs and outputs, between process and result, between investments and returns on the investment. This is precisely why learning is capable of transforming education into an economic transaction, as indicated by Biesta: it focuses on the thingification of learning (its commodification).

It is against this generalizable law of learning that we can return to self-slander as a tactical interruption. When a student engages in self-slander such as "I can't do such and such because I am too stupid," the student is engaged in a rather insufficient tactical interruption of the law of learning which is predicated on actualizing growth, development, or progress through the measuring outcomes. "I can't" opens a paradox within learning: I have learned enough to know that I cannot learn! A cleavage within learning opens that reveals how learning itself cannot fulfill its own law (to assess growth, development, or progress). Indecision is inserted back into the law of learning that undoes its ability to judge or evaluate growth, development, or progress. "I can't" is therefore akin to the kind of self-slander which K. used against the law. In both cases, a paradox is exposed which purportedly stalls the functioning of the juridical (regulative) apparatus at its very heart.

Yet, in an educational setting, such a statement merely empowers the teacher to respond, "Of course you are not stupid, you can do it!" Here we have a re-inscription of the law of learning back into the moment of indistinction opened up by self-slander of the student. Learning is reinscribed precisely through the accusations against the self. The teacher uses the self-slander as a springboard for reassuring the student that he or she not only *can* do the assignment or *is* good at math but that he or she *must* actualize this ability to disprove the charges. Stated differently, the teacher understands that if the student has learned enough to know he or she cannot learn, then learning is still possible, but only through extra effort and pedagogical intervention. In this sense, the teacher transforms the act of self-slander against the law into a new foundation for the law of learning—a law that demands the student self-actualize the required ability despite protests.

In this sense, the student's political and economic gesture to arrest the growth, development, or progress of learning ends with being captured back within the law of learning. Is there no escape? Is there no exodus from the law of learning (as the economization of education)?

Agamben argues that study is an alternative political strategy to self-slander. Again, Kafka is a great example of this. The man from the country who stands before the door to the law in the fable titled "Before the Law" is not killed as was Joseph K. in *The Trial*, instead he outlives the law and returns home. Kafka writes:

> Before the Law stands a doorkeeper. A man from the country comes to this doorkeeper and requests admittance to the Law. But the doorkeeper says that he can't grant him admittance now. The man thinks it over and then asks if he'll be allowed to enter later. 'It's possible,' says the doorkeeper, 'but not now' [...] The doorkeeper gives him a stool and lets him sit down at the side of the door. He sits there for days and years. He asks time and again to be admitted and wearies the doorkeeper with his entreaties. The doorkeeper often conducts brief interrogations, inquiring about his home and many other matters, but he asks such questions indifferently, as great men do, and

in the end he always tells him he still can't admit him [...] Over the many years, the man observes the doorkeeper almost incessantly. He forgets the other doorkeepers and this first one seems to him the only obstacle to his admittance to the Law [...] He curses his unhappy fate, loudly during the first years, later, as he grows older, merely grumbling to himself. He turns childish, and since he has come to know even the fleas in the doorkeeper's collar over his years of study, he asks the fleas to help him change the doorkeeper's mind. Finally his eyes grow dim and he no longer knows whether it's really getting darker around him or if his eyes are merely deceiving him. And yet in the darkness he now sees a radiance that streams forth from the door of the Law. He doesn't have much longer to live now [...] The doorkeeper sees that the man is nearing his end, and in order to reach his failing hearing, he roars at him: 'No one else could gain admittance here, because this entrance was meant solely for you. I'm going to go and shut it now.'[10]

While some might interpret this fable in terms of the victory of the law over the man from the country, Agamben reads it differently. He argues, "If it is true that the door's very openness constituted, as we saw, the invisible power and specific 'force' of the law, then it is possible to imagine that the entire behavior of the man from the country is nothing other than a complicated and patient strategy to have the door closed in order to interrupt the law's being in force."[11] On this reading, it is not that the man is simply doing nothing while he stands before the door of the law. Rather, this is a patient tactic for the door to close that, in the end, works. The man's gesture is an action that seems to achieve nothing. It is an action that does not act. And this strange action is another tactic against the law besides self-slander. Agamben summarizes, "what is

---

10   Franz Kafka, *The Trial*, trans. Breon Mitchell (New York: Schocken Books, 1998), 215-217.

11   Agamben, *Potentialities*, 174.

here at stake is not the study of the law [...] but rather the 'long study of its doorkeeper' [...] to which the man from the country dedicates himself uninterruptedly during his sojourn before the law. It is thanks to this study, to this new Talmud, that the man from the country—in opposition to Josef K.— was able to live to the very end outside the trial."[12] All the man from the country had to do to gain entrance to the law was to engage in an act of self-slander (like Josef K.), yet he preferred not to. Instead, he studied.

But what is study, and how is this different from the strategy of self-slander? In the next section, I will investigate this question, which will reveal the politics of study. I will then conclude with a more detailed analysis of the insufficiencies of self-slander as a political tactic.

STUDY AND SELF-POTENTIALIZATION

Studying is an impotential act. What does an impotential act amount to? How can impotentiality pass completely into an act? An example of an impotential act for Agamben is saying "I can." Here it is worthwhile recounting a story which Agamben tells about the poet Anna Akhmatova:

> In an exergue to the collection of poems she entitled *Requiem*, Anna Akhmatova recounts how her poems were born. It was in the 1930s, and for months and months she joined the line outside the prison of Leningrad, trying to hear news of her son, who had been arrested on political grounds. There were dozens of other women in line with her. One day, one of these women recognized her and, turning to her, addressed her with the following simple question: 'Can you speak of this?' Akhmatova was silent for a moment and then, without knowing how or why, found an answer to the question: 'Yes,' she said, 'I can.'[13]

12   Agamben, *Nudities*, 31.

13   Agamben, *Potentialities*, 177.

There are many important points to unpack in this citation. First off, the experience of her potentiality to do something came out of a devastating horror which left her without
a son and perhaps without much hope. And yet, somehow, she
found within herself a capacity to say, "I can." Almost a rejoin-
der to Adorno's injunction against writing poetry after Aus-
chwitz, Akhmatova's slow yet steady pronunciation has a defi-
ant ring to it. She does not engage in an act of self-slander by
saying something like "I don't have the strength or the knowledge." Instead, she proclaims her potentiality to do something
despite not knowing exactly how or why she will be capable
of doing it. She makes a claim she has no justification for or
right to yet does it anyway. In this sense, the necessity of her
situation is disrupted precisely because of the improbability of
a potentiality where it does not belong. The law—or in this
case, the abject horror of her condition—cannot adequately
respond to this proclamation.

Yet it is important to note that Akhmatova does not
commit to doing something when she says, "I can." The "I
can" cannot be equated with "I will." Instead, an ambivalence
sets in: "I can" announces an ability to do something without committing to the doing of the thing announced. "I can"
does not point beyond itself toward a completed act (a labor, a
work, or a deed), but rather *points back to its own potentiality.*
In this sense, "I can" becomes an impotential act—an act that
does not negate or destroy impotentiality in order to bring
potentiality into being (as a labor, a work, or a deed) but rather
manifests this impotentiality directly. And for this reason, "I
can" is unmeasurable. To say "I can" is a strange act. It is a
kind of happening where nothing happens, or a happening in

which nothing happens except the potentiality for happening. As such, privileging potentiality does not mean that we abandon actuality. Instead, it enables a rethinking of actuality freed from teleological destiny (freed from an end), from the need to fulfill or complete a function, purpose, or vocation. And once this is done, potentiality itself can manifest itself as itself.

But there is something else that is essential to point out about this passage. As Agamben writes, Akhmatova "was silent for a moment." She was contemplating her potentiality for an impossible act. It is my argument that when contemplation is prolonged, it becomes a form of educational life: study. Study is not actually the study of this or that topic or subject but rather a thinking of thought's potentiality to think—a hitting upon the writing tablet of thought. It is a discovery of an "I can x." Instead of an activity which is oriented toward an end, the studier, according to Agamben "does not even desire one."[14] We can understand this in two ways. First, study does not desire a telos or predetermined end. In this sense, when we prioritize potentiality over actuality, then we also prioritize means over ends, use over purposes. Second, we can read this as rejecting any idea of closure.

Agamben argues that there is something "interminable" about studying.[15] If it lacks a destiny (a telos) then learning is released from ends, or the ends become inoperative. For this reason, we might say that studying is inoperative learning, or learning that is separated from its own law of measure. In learning something, a person actualizes an ability so that it can

---

14   Giorgio Agamben, *Idea of Prose*, trans. M. Sullivan and S. Whitsitt (New York: SUNY Press, 1995), 65.

15   Ibid., 64.

be assessed (to determine if it is a success or a failure, to determine if a purpose was met or a telos fulfilled). The potentiality for an activity must pass without remainder into the action. In this sense, the potentiality *not to do* something is sacrificed. Nothing can remain in potentiality. In education, knowledge learned must be made into knowledge evaluated. Learning concerns outcomes—or what comes out of a process. This is precisely the law of learning: one can *and one will* produce evidence of one's potentiality to grow, develop, or improve.

Yet when one studies, what is actualized cannot be measured. Instead of potentiality passing without remainder into the act, we have impotentiality itself pass into the act in the form of thinking one's capacity for thinking (or, in Akhmatova's case, thinking her capacity for making).

And this is extremely important. In the essay "On What We Can Not Do" Agamben argues that the greatest crisis today is an overwhelming sense of hubris in what one *can* do. He argues, "Separated from his [sic] impotentiality, deprived of the experience of what he cannot do, today's man believes himself capable of everything, and so he repeats his jovial 'no problem,' and his irresponsible 'I can do it,' precisely when he should instead realize that he has been consigned in unheard of measure to forces and processes over which he has lost all control."[16] At first, it might seem that Agamben is contradicting himself here. On the one hand, he praises Akhmatova's "I can" and on the other hand he criticizes the neoliberal "I can." Is there a difference here? I would argue yes. Before Akhmatova responded "I can," she "was silent for a moment." This silence and this prolonged hesitation speak to a humility rather

16   Agamben, *Nudities*, 44.

than hubris. It speaks to a prolongation of contemplation, a suspension of ends rather than a self-assured rush to actualize results in the form of a work, a labor, or a deed. Really, the neoliberal "I can" is an "Of course I will... and no one will tell me differently." It contains within itself a sense of confidence, privilege, and willful power. Thus, the neoliberal individual attempts to cleave "I can" from "I cannot" so that the self co-incides without remainder to what it does. The self becomes synonymous with its actualization and thus fully measurable in relation to its outcomes. This logic underlies the learning society and its reification process through which learning and laboring can merge into a single edu-economic logic. Yet Akhmatova's "I can" seems to withdraw from such certainty at the very moment it announces itself. Perhaps there is even a desire to hold onto this impotential remnant as if to hold onto a freedom from certain regulative laws that might measure her abilities against her results. And this is made audible in her utterance "I can."

The Studious Classroom

Here we can return again to the classroom. The studier proclaims, "I can" and in doing so suspends assessment. The outcomes cannot be evaluated, the type of pedagogical inter-vention cannot be determined, progress or regress are neutral-ized. In this sense, the studier is precisely the one standing before the door of the law instead of Josef K.

So instead of self-slander, when a student says "I can" he or she acknowledges an ability but in such a way as to inter-rupt the law of learning which always demands that the "I can" becomes an "I will" or "I will not." If a student says, "I will," the student has accepted the law of learning and will be sub-servient to its command. The teacher knows that an outcome will be produced which can then be evaluated. Thus, the law is obeyed by both student and teacher. If the student resists and says, "I will not," likewise the law can interpret the student's words as indicating a particular reaction—in this case, resis-tance—with its own outcomes (punishment). In both cases, the law is *activated*. In the first, it is obeyed and in the second, it is resisted. And with both of these actions, the law knows what to do: teach and evaluate the learning.

Even if the student said "I can't" and thus engaged in self-slander, the law can respond in due course. If a student says, "I can't," the teacher is able to intervene and *teach* in order to fill in the gap and plaster over the paradox opened up. In this sense, "I can't" is perhaps the most desirable thing a student can say precisely because it opens a space for pedagog-ical intervention. As in Agamben's analysis of Kafka, "I can't" becomes a new foundation for the law—this time, the law of learning. Such slander activates the law by putting the student and teacher into a relation of dependency where the teacher has precisely what can help the student overcome his or her impotence and *learn* something. In all three cases, the actions of the student are caught in the power of the law.

But when the student says, "I can," the law does not know how to react. Remember that to say "I can" does not mean one will or will not do something. "I can" is an impotential act *in itself*, full stop, without reference to an outcome (indeed it does not even desire one). In short, the phrase shifts from obe-dience, resistance, or self-slander to self-potentialization. For instance, if I (as a teacher) approached a student and asked her to revise a failed essay, and the student simply says, "I can do that," at first, I might be relieved and even thankful. Yet upon deeper reflection, I might be troubled by this phrase. Did the student mean that she *will* do it or simply that she *can* do it? There is something *indeterminate* about the response that opens up the possibility of contingency (the student might prefer not to do the requested revisions even though she can). Further, the pronunciation of "I can" seems to speak to a level of agency and preparedness that no longer calls for pedagogical oversight. If the student had said "I can't" then I would know exactly what to do: reassure her that she *can*, that I can help, that I can enact my role as a teacher to make sure that she accomplishes the set task. In short, the attempt at self-slander merely reinscribes the student back into the circuits of the law of learning, and therefore keeps open the space and time for pedagogical and/or psychological intervention. Yet to say "I can" is disturbing as it leaves no room for the teacher, and in this sense, *deactivates* the law of learning.

To say "I can" as an act of self-potentialization does not re-inscribe the law nor does it destroy the law. It suspends the law for a moment. As a teacher faced with the phrase "I can," I am thrown off my game. The student has not obeyed me (as the legislator of the law of learning), nor has she offended me by refusing my command. Instead, she has merely proclaimed her ability to do something (which is not the same as guaranteeing she will do something). She refuses to submit her potentiality to actuality (and thus negate impotentiality) without giving offence. Offence is the pitting of one will against another will and thus involves relations of force. Yet "I can" does not exert such force. This is a positive act of self-potentialization, which nevertheless does not actualize anything other than its own potentiality (nor does it promise to fulfill this potentiality in the form of a specific outcome). And yet, the law seems momentarily paralyzed by this sudden appearance of a potentiality which it cannot control or measure.

If "I can't" as self-slander seemed weak, then it was not weak enough in that its weakness reinvigorates the law of learning to take further action. A truly weak response to the law is to say "I can" full stop, leaving the law with hanging questions concerning the meaning of this: Will there be an outcome to be verified? If so, when will it come? Does the student need help or does he have it under control? Should I intervene or not? Such questions interrupt the function of the law to capture potentiality in a form that is measurable. But what is left of education if there is no teacher teaching and no learner learning?

FROM RELATIONS TO POINTS OF CONTACT

These questions appear whenever there is an impotentiality manifested in an act. Instead of forcing the student to learn or punishing the student for not learning, what if the teacher simply opened up the space and time in the classroom for contemplation to become a form of educational life? What if the utterance "I can" were allowed to linger and thus become an opportunity for study rather than for learning? When the student says, "I can," she opens a space and time for the study of potentiality that separates and joins teachers and students. On the student side, she can contemplate her potentiality to do something (and not to do something). Study grows out of contemplation, and in turn, is the contemplation of the potentiality to contemplate. And through this act, the student self-potentializes the self by stumbling upon a primordial "I can x." Another way of putting this is that she contemplates what freedom remains in an educational form of life which is continually divided against itself through learning (divided in terms of before and after, ignorant and knowledgeable). This is the freedom to "I can x" without the imperative to actualize this "I can" into a definitive, measurable form of assessment (growth, development, or progress).

For the teacher "I cannot" means jumping into action, but "I can" is more paradoxical and causes a longer hesitation. This hesitation, if prolonged further, can institute a different understanding of what a teacher does *by not doing anything*—an inoperative kind of teaching, or teaching whose gestures are liberated from always having to enforce the law of learning. When the student says, "I can," the teacher, in turn, can study her own impotentiality to teach and not to teach. When the student says, "I can," the relation between teacher and student within the law of learning is suspended, but the teacher does not have to disappear. Rather, he or she remains but in a suspended state that is in exodus from the law of learning which binds both the student and teacher to a specific logic: the logic of regulating processes of learning and verifying outcomes. In this state, the teacher is faced with his or her own impotentiality to and not to teach.

In this sense, opening the space and time for study offered up when the student says "I can" shifts the nature of the student-teacher relationship. Indeed, it is no longer even a relationship. According to Agamben, relationship as an ontological category is problematic as it always emerges from the presupposition of at least two different identities that must be put into relation. In learning relations, these identities are often formulated according to the immature and the mature, the ignorant and the knowledgeable, and so forth. These pairs are always defined in terms of an opposition. For instance, self-slander ("I can't") simultaneously (a) presupposes the division between ignorance and knowledge and (b) enacts this division. Yet when a student proclaims "I can" even if he or she has no right to, suddenly a potentiality is made manifest that disrupts the division. Therefore, Agamben can argue that potentiality "is capable of always deposing ontological-political relations in order to cause a contact [...] to appear in their elements."[17] *Contact* is a kind of relational non-relation, or an inoperative relationship where the division divides itself. This is a zone that is indescribable using the language of relations and is beyond the language of educational outcomes. This contact touches that which is presupposed by relationality but never thematized: potentiality (to do and not to do something, to be and not to be someone).

"I can," if taken seriously, suspends the law of learning, refuses relation, and instead opens a new form of educational life where students and teachers can come into contact through study. I am not arguing this will happen, but it is a possibility which is not possible when a student says, "I will," or "I will not," or "I can't." And this simple "I can" is the most precious—but also the most precarious—gift (for both the student and the teacher).

---

17   Giorgio Agamben, *Use of Bodies*, trans. A. Kotsko (Stanford: Stanford University Press, 2016), 272.

PART IV

Antifascist and Anticapitalist Education

CHAPTER 9

The Taste of Antifascist Art Education

In his book *Late Marxism*, Fredric Jameson persuasively argues that Theodor Adorno's negative dialectic is a vital and necessary tool to combat the ludic tendencies of postmodernism.[1] Jameson's intervention is timely, rehabilitating Adorno from contemporary historians and theorists who either position him as a cantankerous curmudgeon or relegate his thought to a depoliticized if not reactionary aesthetic realm. Opposed to both perspectives, Jameson repositions Adorno as the theorist of late capitalism whose pessimism acts as a sobering agent against the intoxication of market desire and against postmodernity's perpetual present.

While I agree with Jameson that Adorno is in fact a central figure in our postmodern times for imagining a politics of anticapitalism, I would also argue that Jameson, in his assessment of Adorno's work, has somewhat missed his mark.

---

1   Fredric Jameson, *Late Marxism* (London: Verso, 2000). Paper presented at the 8th Biennial Radical Philosophy Association Conference, University of San Francisco, San Francisco, 2009.

Keeping Jameson's basic thesis in mind, we must now turn to Adorno's theory of education to see how his project remains relevant to the present historical moment. To clarify this argument, I will bridge the gap between Adorno's aesthetic theory and his education theory through the mediation of art education, which will become a primary location from which to address the question of fascist resentment. Ending fascist resentment is a new educational and ethical mandate precisely because fascism is the psychological logic of late capitalism whose most gruesome and barbaric manifestation is genocide.

A Shared Problematic:
The Precarious Position of the Philistine

To begin, Jameson carefully documents three different social types in Adorno's text *Aesthetic Theory*.[2] First is the position of the laboring masses. Here Jameson connects *Aesthetic Theory* with *The Dialectic of Enlightenment*,[3] which provides us with the most succinct allegorical representation of this position: Odysseus's crew, who cannot hear the call of the sirens because their ears are plugged with wax. In other words, Odysseus' oarsmen know that aesthetic experience exists, but are excluded from entering the aesthetic realm by their location in the social relations of production. Second, *Aesthetic Theory* critiques the consumers of the culture industry. Barred from directly experiencing the promised happiness of the aes-

---

2   Theodor Adorno, *Aesthetic Theory*, trans. R. Hullot-Kentor (Minneapolis: University of Minnesota Press, 1998).

3   Max Horkheimer and Theodor W. Adorno, *Dialectic of Enlightenment: Philosophical Fragments*, trans. E. Jephcott (Stanford: Stanford University Press, 2007).

thetic realm, these individuals indulge in the false pleasures of mass-produced commodities. Such pleasures mystify social contradictions and thus perform a convenient function in the reproduction of labor power: momentary escapism.

Yet for Jameson, there exists another antagonist in *Aesthetic Theory* whose challenge to aesthetics proves the most challenging: the philistine. As opposed to the non-hearing oarsman or the consumer of the culture industry, the philistine understands art, and for this very reason is full of resentment towards its broken promise of happiness. The key connection between Adorno's aesthetics and his more overtly political critique of enlightenment how becomes clear, for as Jameson argues in *Late Marxism*, the central figure of the philistine is in fact the anti-Semitic Nazi. The fascist, in other words, is envious of the broken promise of art, which in the end amounts to a utopian hope for social transformation. This envy leads to an increasing resentment and to the process of revolt against the concept of happiness, resulting in a distortion of happiness with power.[4] Perhaps we can argue that philistinism is the *taste* of the fascist who lusts for happiness only through the violence of power.

For our present purposes, what is most important in Jameson's insights is that we can now precisely locate a necessary bridge between aesthetics and education: the shared problematic of the taste of the philistine for resentment through power and the power of resentment for the fascist. Although Adorno's *Aesthetic Theory* posits the philistine as an antagonist, the text offers no solution to addressing this politically dangerous figure. Rather, the book merely negates the position.

---

4   Horkheimer and Adorno, *Dialectic of Enlightenment*, 141.

Adorno's educational proposals, on the other hand, attempt to provide a direct, critical intervention. If his aesthetic theory remains austere (strategically addressed to those who have already cultivated a set of shared tastes and as such are already educationally prepared for the impact of an aesthetic experience), Adorno's educational program is geared at combating the spread of fascism throughout the cultural and politics spheres from the ground up. Stated differently, if as Adorno once argued, "[A]rt becomes social by its opposition to society, and occupies this position only as autonomous art," then perhaps we could argue the inverse for education: pedagogical practice is oppositional to society because it engages directly in the everyday life-world.[5]

The two problems of aesthetics and education are thus dialectical inversions of one another but also intimately interwoven. The two work together in order to prevent the resentment toward happiness found in philistinism from turning into full-blown fascist ideology. As Adorno writes, "school today, its moral import, is that in the midst of the status quo it alone has the ability, if it is conscious of it, to work directly toward the debarbarization of humanity."[6] Education *alone* has this ability. Whatever ability art has to aid in this process of debarbarization is dependent upon this more basic educational operation. I want to highlight the great importance that Adorno attributes to education in an antifascist struggle, yet I would also suggest that there is a missed articulation here between

---

5   Adorno, *Aesthetic Theory*, 225.

6   Theodor Adorno, *Critical Models: Interventions and Catchwords*, trans. H. Pickford (New York: Columbia University Press, 2005), 190.

education and aesthetic experience: *art education*. The goal of the rest of this paper is to close the gap between education and aesthetic experience in order to see how we must think the two together in a dialectical tension in order to "solve" the complex problem of fascism through the seemingly apolitical problem of philistine taste. The paradoxical result is as follows: art education becomes oppositional to society because of how the seemingly apolitical and disinterested autonomy of art is brought to bear on the formation of aesthetic sensibilities in children.

ADORNO'S ANTIFASCIST EDUCATIONAL PHILOSOPHY

For Adorno, fascism is an intensification of the most basic aesthetic tastes found in bourgeois philistinism: tastes that are hard and cold. Hardness makes the subject resistant to pain and likewise resistant to the guilt of inflicting pain on others. Self and other become essentially objects to be manipulated, resulting in a "reified consciousness" wherein human relationships become relationships between things.[7] In this sense, hardness is a taste for techno-rational and instrumental logics of the enlightenment itself—so brutally prefigured in Odysseus who tied himself to the mast in order to hear the call of the sirens without the pleasures of sensual fulfillment.[8] Likewise, coldness speaks to an indifference to others and a sense of isolation through an insatiable taste for competition, and ultimately, domination.

The result is a manipulative consciousness that is characterized by "a rage for organization, by the inability to have

7   Adorno, *Critical Models*, 199.

8   Horkheimer and Adorno, *Dialectic of Enlightenment.*

any immediate human experiences at all, by a certain lack of emotion, by an overvalued realism."[9] As such, the tastes of the philistine are anti-dialectical, fully one-dimensional, devoid of emotional resonance with others, and incapable of recognizing the non-identical in the identical, or the penetration of subject and object. In sum, hardness and coldness are aesthetic propensities that equate happiness with manipulation, power, and resentment, generating the preconditions for fascist political ideology—in all its militarized and patriotic forms. Although philistines understand art, they turn their backs on it out of spite, entrenching themselves in the very coldness and hardness that is antithetical to the dialectics of aesthetic experience.

If *art* education is able to pierce the crusted psyche of hardness and coldness inherent in our commodified world, then it adequately produces the preconditions for an antifascist aesthetic experience of self and other. According to Adorno, aesthetic perception enables us to reflect on social suffering that is prohibited by hardness and coldness. Thus, Adorno writes, "Hegel's thesis that art is consciousness of plight has been confirmed beyond anything he could have envisioned."[10] Through art, personal pain and suffering become a social and historical issue, and individual emotions enter a larger narrative of collective suffering that cannot be falsely massaged into the pre-packaged pleasures of the culture industry or the indifference of coldness and hardness. Here aesthetic perception emerges as a crucial moment within an overall educational problematic centered against fascism. The arc from education to aesthetics resists reification of consciousness into a thing,

---

9   Adorno, *Aesthetic Theory*, 198.

10   Ibid., 18.

opening up the subject to its own constitutive "plight" within a given historical context.

Importantly, it is precisely the lack of overt political content in art that makes it political. The autonomy of art must be preserved, for it is in this autonomy that the broken promise of happiness can transform into a critical evaluation of the present historical moment as an obstacle needing to be overcome. Adorno writes, "The unsolved antagonisms of reality return in artworks as immanent problems of form."[11] Take for instance abstract art. It appears to have no social content at all, nor does it seem to represent any political ideology. For all intents and purposes, it asserts its "autonomy" from such matters. Yet, for Adorno, abstract art is only autonomous from society insofar as it mimetically reflects society's own abstractness (everything is subsumed within exchange value). The autonomy of art does not mean that it is divorced from social, economic, and political pressures outside of it. Indeed, the autonomy of art is dependent on social, economic, and political pressures. Yet art can *know* these pressures—and in turn, expose them—precisely by taking them up within itself in mediated form. Art's autonomy is a symptom of its heteronomy!

Art's autonomy is a scar. A scar is an historical index to past conflicts that never fully heal. There is always a trace of difference lingering in a scar that cannot be fully subsumed within the self. The wound never leaves, yet the scar is like a material mark of a promise of happiness (healing, resolution, regeneration, wholeness) even if this happiness is unfulfilled. "Scars of damage and disruption are the modern's seal of authenticity; by their means, art desperately negates the closed

---

11   Ibid., 6.

confines of the ever-same; explosion is one of its invariants."[12] Unlike the hardness and coldness of the philistine who resents this unfulfilled promise of happiness, art offers a weak (yet oddly powerful) response: open the self up to its otherness (the scar) that marks it as non-identical but in a nonviolent and non-domineering way (as opposed to the fascist, who merely negates, excluded, or exploits otherness).

Conclusion:
Adorno's Antifascist Art Education for Today

In conclusion, art education is charged with the vital role of preventing the rise of barbarism by cracking open the reified crust of hardness and coldness defining the psychological makeup of the philistine, and by extension the fascist. It must replace hardness and coldness with an openness of the subject towards the other (both within and without) in a nonviolent moment of aesthetic experience. With this openness, art education moves from a model of resentment (in which the other must be negated) towards a model of aesthetic perception capable of dislodging the narrowing of perception and affect into fascist channels. Such a position flies in the face of the two antagonistic trends in art education today. On the one hand, we have the rise of "critical art education" which puts art in the service of political projects and political slogans. On the other hand, in reaction to this trend, we are witnessing a retreat into formalist aesthetics. The first pole vaults art into the political sphere (thus art's autonomy is lost), while the second asserts the autonomy of art while misrecognizing how art is political precisely because of its autonomy. It is not clear

---

12   Ibid., 23.

that either of these approaches is adequate to the task at hand: cultivating antifascist taste for the non-identical. Indeed, they might very well lead to variations on the theme of philistinism (one leading to resentment toward art as a mere ideological, instrumental weapon and the other leading to resentment toward art as an elitist, detached, and thus dead canon of great works). Opposed to either position we find Adorno who argues that art education needs to maintain the autonomy of art in order to cultivate a new sense of aesthetic taste capable of overcoming the hard and cold taste of the philistine (as this lies at the heart of the social psychology of the fascist).

CHAPTER 10

Why Read Walter Benjamin Today?

In this talk, I am going to try to summarize the central themes and basic structure of my book *Walter Benjamin's Antifascist Education: From Riddles to Radio*.[1] What might be surprising to some is that Benjamin was first and foremost an educational philosopher and activist. Under the influence of the progressive practice of Gustav Wyneken which focused on anti-authoritarian, nonhierarchical models of education, Benjamin started writing about educational reform, youth, and the theme of awakening as a high school student in Berlin. Later, he became active in the German Youth Movement both in high school and then as a university student in Freiburg and Berlin, ultimately becoming the president of the Berlin University Chapter of the Independent Students' Association.

As of late, there has been a lot of scholarship on the early Benjamin as an educational philosopher, including an ex-

---

1   This paper was presented at a special author-meets-critic session of the International Network for Philosophers of Education, held via zoom in 2022.

cellent edited volume on the topic in the journal *boundary 2*, but my contribution to this body of literature is to show how Benjamin never left these educational concerns behind. Instead, we can read his work as a dispersal of educational themes outward, beyond the schoolhouse and the university into public forms of pedagogy including radio and children's theater, and then even more broadly into informal educational forms such as collecting, wandering the city, laughing at film, until language itself becomes a special kind of "teacher." My book provides a tentative map of this dispersal, taking seriously Benjamin's early statement that "everyone is an educator and everyone needs to be educated and everything is education."[2] The result is, when viewed collectively, what I call a constellational curriculum of various educational forms, each with its own internal educational potentiality.

The central focus of the book is derived from early writings by Benjamin on education as an "awakening" or "threshold" or "wave." In all cases, what binds these descriptions together is an interest in the phenomenon of "swelling." As Benjamin writes, "A Schwelle [threshold] is a zone. Transformation, passage, and wave action are in a word schwellen."[3] It is from this one sentence that I generate the major themes of Benjamin's antifascist pedagogy as well as the fundamental structure of the book. In short, education is a special kind of swell or threshold, and the book as a whole demonstrates how

2   Walter Benjamin, *Gesammelte Briefe, Volume 1*, ed. Christoph Gödde and Henri Lonitz (Frankfurt am Main: Suhrkamp, 1995), 382-83.

3   Walter Benjamin, *The Arcades Project*, eds. H. Eiland and K. McLaughlin (Cambridge, MA: Harvard University Press, 1999), 494.

educational interests swell up and outward, creating a constellational curriculum that sets in relation seemingly unrelated elements of Benjamin's work.

There are three swellings that I examine in relation to education. First, as already indicated, Benjamin defines education as an awakening from the mythic past. I agree with this assertion, but also argue it needs to be further complexified. Awakening itself is a specific kind of swelling that expresses an educational potentiality. Stated briefly, education is an act that makes tradition "visible and free."[4] It is not the negation of traditions or simply their mechanical inheritance but rather the point at which traditions become visible, recognizable, and thus knowable as what they are: products of history.

Second, internal to education is how teaching swells out of learning, as if it were a wave in an ocean. Benjamin writes, "learning has evolved into teaching, in part gradually but wholly from within."[5] In this sense, teaching is just a modification within learning, a modification that swells up out of the rhythms of learning and studying to the point where such practices turn outward into a teaching. Learning makes tradition visible (in its knowability), and teaching makes that which is visible free (in its transmissibility). What is important here, is that both learning and teaching are *interrelated* as educational swelling points. Through learning, that which is knowable in something swells to the surface, and through teaching, this knowability swells up even further to spill outward in the form of texts, notes, lectures, recordings, etc. There are two implications of this. First, teaching is not to be

---

4   Benjamin, *Gesammelted Briefe, Volume 1*, 382-83.

5   Ibid.

defined as a relation between students and teachers as many in the field of education want to suggest. Rather, it is first and foremost an internal relationship between the learner and the transmissibility of what has been learned. Second, there can never really be a professional teacher, as the teacher is merely the most extreme or swollen manifestation of the learner—the learner at his or her most grotesque. Teaching here is not a volitional act, but rather a passive yielding to the swelling up of knowability to the point where it must externalize itself in the form of a teaching (or a thing that has the potentiality to be transmitted). Throughout my book, I chart the ebb and flow of the metaphor of swelling throughout Benjamin's constellational curriculum, highlighting how each educational form offers up its own special kind of educational swelling.

Third, as described above, Benjamin's entire body of work can be seen as the swelling of this educational theme of awakening outward into more and more diverse objects, practices, and technologies. In this sense, the book is an attempt to follow along on this swell, from the moment when awakening makes something knowable through the practice of teaching which makes this knowability free (for others) through the dispersal of the problematic of awakening throughout media culture. The result is a constellational curriculum that holds together seemingly unrelated objects, practices, and media together under the idea of educational life.

Phenomenologically speaking, awakening as an educational swelling point manifests itself in three ways. First, there are mimetic forms in which the body itself swells up with difference through gestural modification or augmentation. Although not covered in the book, one could say that Benjamin's emphasis on mimetic similarities offers a rather shocking intervention into current educational philosophy. Whereas educational philosophy today concerns itself with difference—in the form of identity politics, ontologies of difference, respecting differences, and so on—Benjamin founds education in terms of our ability to find similarities across differences through mimesis. Importantly, mimesis enables the body to touch that which is farthest away and thus to overcome great differences in order to produce resonances/similarities (that are not reducible to differences or identities).

Second, there are innervative kinds of swelling in which the body's internal energy system excites and intensifies itself causing ruptures in sedimented habitual patterns. Whereas much critical pedagogy focuses on beliefs—reflecting critically on one's beliefs, one's biases, and so on[6]—Benjamin turns to the body and how biases are enfleshed. Through innervation—as the excitation of the body through extension and intensification—the body can rupture its habits or reorganize them into a new configuration. Interestingly, this means that unlike other members of the Frankfurt School of critical theory that drew educational resources from Freud and psychoanalysis, Benjamin supplemented the possibility for an embodied education with Russian film theory and its focus on perceptual innervation.[7] And finally, there are distracted kinds of swell-

---

6   See, Tyson E. Lewis, *The Aesthetics of Education: Theatre, Curiosity, and Politics in the Work of Jacques Rancière and Paulo Freire* (London: Continuum, 2012) for a critique of this intellectualist bias in critical pedagogy, especially in the work of Freire.

7   For more details on this topic see Matthew Charles, "Secret Signals from Another World: Walter Benjamin's Theory of Innervation," *New German Critique* 45, no. 3 (2018): 39-72.

ing where perception enlarges itself or opens itself up to that which exceeds focus or attentiveness. Unlike most educational philosophy that focuses on attention, Benjamin attempts to find educational value within distraction itself. In a way he thinks distraction against itself, enabling us to differentiate between educational forms of distraction as open attunement/dispersal (*Zerstreuung*) vs mere diversion/deflection/steering away from (*Ablenkung*) as induced by the culture industry. Indeed, educational philosophers of all kinds, on the right and the left, liberals and radicals, modernists and postmodernists, critics and post-critics all agree that education necessarily includes the cultivation of attentiveness. Yet Benjamin allows us to redeem distraction as educationally important.

In each case (mimesis, innervation, and distraction), swelling is more concerned with transformations on the preconscious level of the body than on conscious thought or beliefs. In this sense, education for Benjamin is decisively affective rather than cognitive or mental. The question then becomes how these precognitive affective interruptions and irritations can themselves swell to the point of conscious knowability and, in turn, become transmissible? Drawing on a distinction that has not received any commentary in the secondary literature on Benjamin, I then argue that studying is the fleeting sensation of swelling while learning is this sensation being made conscious and thus knowable on the level of conceptualization. This terminological distinction between two modes of education relates closely to Benjamin's distinction between two modes of life: *Erlebnis* (short, nondurational, isolated experience) and *Erfarung* (durational, extended experience).

Let me give you one brief example from the book of how

this theory of education swells out of an unlikely and seemingly non-educational practice: wandering through a city. First, Benjamin was fascinated with cities and with traveling through cities. He wrote memoirs of his childhood in Berlin as well as descriptions of his many travels to Naples, Moscow, and so forth. First off, for the traveler, encountering a cityscape for the first time can be a distracting experience. Habits, customs, and ways of getting around no longer function properly. One does not know where to go, what to look at, or how to act. On a deeper level, one's intentionality is also disrupted: one's plans often do not work out and one's interests are often sidetracked. This distraction opens one up to new possibilities for thinking but also for feeling and sensing. It allows the body to become innervated with new sensations derived from one's environment. The body finds itself moving differently through foreign streets, alerted to new sounds, smells, tastes, and so forth. The body encounters the knowability of the city, or what can be known about this city, only by displacing sedimented habits (distraction), and then mimetically taking on the city within itself. The body swells up to meet the city, touching that which is most distant from its familiar ways of being, transforming itself in the process. Benjamin's sudden, unanticipated, pre-conscious studies of the city swell up into a learning (what is knowable about the city) that, in turn, swells up into a teaching (Benjamin's essays) that can be made free for others.

Finally, the real stakes of this book rest not on defining education alone, but on the relevancy of Benjamin today for understanding the crisis of the present. Indeed, I have been wanting to write a book on Benjamin since graduate school, but it was only when certain historical conditions were in place that

I was compelled to write the book. Perhaps one could even say that the book swelled out of me as the result of a kind of personal and political innervation caused by the rise of global, neofascist groups. Indeed, the curricular constellation of educational forms I have drawn together in this book offer up an antifascist form of educational life. While the protofascist authoritarian personality can be defined in terms of hardness, coldness, and manipulativeness, the educational body proposed by Benjamin offers a radical alternative. For instance, hardness shuts the body off from otherness whereas mimesis opens the body up to entanglements with otherness. Coldness freezes over the ability of the body's affective capacities while innervation heightens and exaggerates these capacities. And finally, manipulativeness demands a certain kind of willful focus on controlling power while distraction suspends the will, letting go of any desire to control, and yielding to experience. Such distraction also means that individuals and collectives cannot be manipulated through any kind of centralized authority, as they continually swell up and spill out from defined political ideologies and boundaries. These larger, political implications do not mean that education itself is subsumed within or by political concerns. Instead, politics is another kind of swell that is possible though not inevitable within the waves of studying, learning, and teaching. In this sense, the book thus offers 4 instead of 3 swelling points: the moment of encountering that swells up with an awakening to what is knowable, the swelling of such learning into a teaching, the swelling of teachings into a diasporic constellation, and the swelling of such a constellation into an antifascist politics.

Another way of thinking about the complex relationship

between politics and education is through a messianic lens (as mediated by a theological category). In the notoriously dense aphorism titled "Theologico-Political Fragment" Benjamin writes, "Therefore the Kingdom of God is not the telos of the historical dynamic; it cannot be set as a goal" without ending in disaster.[8] The Kingdom cannot be made into a goal, and profane life cannot be instrumentalized into a means to achieving an end beyond itself. But this does not mean that profane life and the Kingdom have no relationship. Benjamin argues the opposite: "just as a force can, through acting, increase another that is acting in the opposite direction, so the order of the profane assists, through being profane, the coming of the messianic Kingdom."[9] In other words, only by pursuing the profane life as a pure means without turning into a means to an end, can the messianic Kingdom be fulfilled.

We can think here of Marx's classless society as a political end. When profane life is turned into a means to achieving this end, the results are horrific, life turns into totalitarian necropolitics. Instead, the idea of a classless society must never be seen as a telos or goal of politics, and only in this way can it be achieved. I would argue that it is the same with education: antifascist education should never be seen as a goal. To do so would only result in perpetuating fascist education in the name of antifascism. Instead, profane life in the classroom must be a means released from such a telos, and in this sense, remain firmly political by rejecting politicization. And this is

---

8   Walter Benjamin, *Selected Writings, Volume 3, 1935-1938*, eds. H. Eiland and M. W. Jennings (Cambridge, MA: Harvard University Press, 2002), 305.

9   Ibid.

perhaps the most difficult and simple educational response to fascism: not political slogans or movements but rather the gesture of making something knowable and free in its transmissibility.

CHAPTER 11

WALTER BENJAMIN'S PHENOMENOLOGY OF DISTRACTION AS EDUCATIONAL FLASHPOINT

In the field of educational theory today, there is unanimous agreement that education concerns the cultivation of attentiveness.[1] Indeed, distraction is considered a distinct enemy, lacking any educational relevance whatsoever. Thus, a normative dichotomy is set up between distraction (bad) and attention (good). What is interesting about Benjamin is that he shifts our focus from this dichotomy between distraction and attentiveness, toward an internal distinction between two kinds of distraction. It is this internal distinction that, I will argue, is important for thinking about what is educational in flashpoints, or those moments when the preconscious knowledge of the body makes itself known.

On the one hand, Benjamin highlights distraction as mere diversion (*Ablenkung*). This is the typical notion of distraction

---

1   This paper was delivered at the Philosophy of Education Society Meeting in San Jose, CA, 2022.

criticized in educational literature. Such diversion is associated by Benjamin with our fascination with images, our captivation by commodities, and our indulgence in the phantasmagoria of modern living. This kind of diversion is also heavily criticized by critical theorists such as Horkheimer and Adorno in their analysis of the culture industry as lulling the masses to sleep, preventing them from paying attention to their exploitation.[2] For example, citing the poet Baudelaire, Benjamin refers to the first department stores as shrines embodying the "religious intoxication of great cities."[3] Further, Benjamin describes the world's fair as a "phantasmagoria which a person enters in order to be distracted."[4] In both cases, the captivated spectator of department stores and world's fairs is held in throng by "*divertissements*"—a neologism that combines diversion with advertisement—that do not sell particular items so much as a consumptive, divertive lifestyle.[5] But most importantly, Benjamin highlights that the germinal seed for all these various diversions that now make up our collective lives within a media saturated culture lies in the commodity itself.

The commodity as such offers the "glitter of distractions" as its main feature.[6] This means that the commodity is the atomic unit of all subsequent diversions, deflecting workers away from the class struggle, thus supporting the perfect illusion of access, entertainment, and ease offered up by a consum-

2   See Horkheimer and Adorno on the culture industry in *Dialectic of Enlightenment*.

3   Benjamin, *The Arcades Project*, 16.

4   Ibid.

5   Ibid.

6   Ibid., 18.

erist dream. For instance, commodities are produced through human labor power, yet when they enter into circulation, they seem to become animated by their own, internal, supernatural energies. Commodities are therefore *haunted* by the labor power that created them, but also, they actively mediate between humans in the public sphere, transforming immediate recognition into distorted projections of capitalist design.

All of this might sound relatively familiar to critical theorists as well as educators who are leery of distraction and therefore attempt to overcome it by cultivating the virtues of attention. But this is only one half of a complicated story. For Benjamin there is also a positive and productive kind of distraction, or what might be thought of as horizontal, nondiscriminating openness to whatever appears (*Zerstreuung*).[7] In this state of distraction, one is not attentive to any one particular thing, but rather receptive to experiences that might fall outside of one's sphere of attentiveness. Thus, this positive notion of distraction holds open the possibility that perceptual rules dividing what can from what cannot be seen are suspended, allowing a radical moment where (1) something new can appear and through this appearance (2) alter the cognitive-perceptual relation, which itself now incorporates difference and alterity.

These two kinds of distraction map on to two distinct experiences of shock found in Benjamin's work. Negative shocks, as in the shock of the city, are paralyzing and rigidifying for Benjamin. They are the shocks experienced by the anonymous

---

7   For more on this distinction see Carolin Duttlinger, "Between Contemplation and Distraction: Configurations of Attention in Walter Benjamin," *German Studies Review* 30, no. 1 (2007): 33-54.

crowds described in the poetry of Baudelaire. These shocks are mere diversions. But Benjamin also discusses the ability of certain shocks to educate. These shocks are associated with the sudden appearance of dialectical images. Dialectical images are described by Benjamin using the imagery of thunderclaps and lightning. The force of the dialectical image comes from this flash, which I am arguing is a productive distraction, a temporary disorientation from our normal bodily habits, ways of seeing, and perceiving. It *denaturalizes* the way things are, the order of things, the partitioning of the sensible that defines the present. We suddenly encounter the invisible within the visible, or forces that exceed our interest. The thunderclap and flash of the image indicate that illumination happens first and foremost through an innervation in our bodily energies and capacities, fundamentally expanding what it is a body can sense.

To return to the topic at hand, Benjamin's notion of productive distraction is thus important for educational philosophy, for it is only through a momentary, disorienting "flash" of a dialectical image that some kind of awakening is possible (or rather a heightening of sensorial awareness, an opening up of the body to extended and intensified perceptual capacities). The unexpected thunderclap and lightning flash of the dialectical image stop us in our tracks, throw us off balance, cause a glitch in our sensorial apprehension of ourselves, our bodies, and our environments. In terms of educational practice, this means sensitizing students and ourselves to moments of distraction, allowing ourselves to be open to the flash of the flashpoint, being open and receptive to the possibility that the flash might offer us its own, unique kind of knowledge. This also means accepting that education is not simply about attentiveness, but also about breaking attentiveness when necessary, in order to see beyond that which our attentiveness holds to be relevant or important. Instead, it is possible that distraction itself holds a plenitude of experiences that exceed attentiveness's focus. In conclusion, I offer a provocative hypothesis: education is not poor in attentiveness. In education we find *too much* attentiveness. Students are not suffering from attention deficit disorder so much as attention surplus disorder.[8] To teach for profane illumination would thus open a new educational problematic, one that reminds us that education might just happen on the periphery of perception where events, things, sensations can "grab" attention with an explosive force of a thunderclap, shattering its hold over experience, and thus open us up to new possibilities for recognizing something about ourselves that would otherwise remain invisible.

---

8   Susan Sontag cited in Jill Krementz, *The Writer's Desk* (New York: Random House, 1996), 17.

CHAPTER 12

Constant Contact

One might argue that the problem of contact is a prob-lem of the ratio between nearness and distance.[1] At best, contact implies a certain nearness, or potential to draw near, while also suggesting the possibility that a certain amount of distance could be inserted into this nearness—that one could lose contact. And if this is the case, then the concept of "con-stant contact" might suggest a disequilibrium in the ratio of nearness and distance, if not an eclipse of the very possibility of distancing. For instance, if one is in a state of constant con-tact, then how could one possibly unplug, disengage, or turn off the stream of contacts that one is constantly bombarded with? I am thinking here of my own experience with email, and my students' constant demand for contact. Or, I am also thinking of my subjection to a barrage of aggressive speech

---

1   This paper was delivered at the Philosophy of Education Soci-ety Meeting in San Jose, CA, 2022 in response to the conference theme of "contact zones."

from alt-right and neo-Nazi groups several years ago because of an article on whiteness I had published. In this case, the most effective weapon of intimidation was the threat of constant contact with me through social media.[2]

In this short paper, I want to analyze this problem with reference to a little discussed early essay by Walter Benjamin titled "On the Psychophysical Problem."[3] Although written in the 1920s, I feel it offers a unique analysis of nearness and distance that is useful today in the age of "constant contact." At one point in the essay, Benjamin turns toward nearness and distance as "two factors that may be as important for the structure and life of the body as other spatial categories (up and down, right and left, etcetera)."[4] For Benjamin, nearness and distance are foundational to understanding the lived experience of individual bodies, and although he links them to spatiality, this spatiality is decisively existential, phenomenological, perceptual, and epistemological in nature. For instance, he argues that stupidity is a kind of intellectual or epistemological form of nearness to the content of thought. Stupidity is an "all-too-close (mindless) examination of ideas" or captivation by the beauty of ideas without any critical distance.[5] In such cases, humans are imprisoned by what lies nearest at

2   See Lewis, *Walter Benjamin's Antifascist Education* for more details related to this experience.

3   For a more detailed overview of this important essay, see Eli Friedlander, *Walter Benjamin: A Philosophical Portrait* (Cambridge, MA: Harvard University Press, 2012).

4   Walter Benjamin, *Selected Writings, Volume 1, 1913-1926*, eds. M. Bullock and M. W. Jennings (Cambridge, MA: Belknap Press, 2004), 397.

5   Ibid., 397.

hand, trapped by a certain myopic approach to the world in which only the closest things, ideas, people, and so forth matter. The individual comes to be *determined* by what is near at hand. This closeness seems to extinguish the very possibility of thinking, in the sense that the individual is consumed by that which is all-too-close. Such reactivity does not offer the space needed for critical assessment, or better yet, any kind of *distraction* from the gravitational pull of that which lies nearest at hand, what is most identifiable, familiar, and accessible.

The opposite can be found in figures such as Nietzsche. Benjamin writes, "Nietzsche's life is typical for someone who is determined wholly by distance."[6] Nietzsche is untimely, or out of touch with what is near. Thus, his audience is in the future, those who are at a decisive distance from the norms, values, and ideologies binding others' to the present moment. In this sense, Nietzsche is not stupid, yet at the same time, Nietzsche cannot have any relationship to that which is closest and cannot approach what is near. For this very reason, "whatever comes close to them is uncontrolled" and that which comes close assumes a "terrible form."[7] Although Benjamin gestures toward Nietzsche's incapacity for achieving sexual intimacy, we can also think of Nietzsche's terrifying and ultimately debilitating confrontation with a horse whose pain from being whipped got to close to handle, leading to an absolute breakdown from which he could not recover. It is difficult not to think of Nietzsche when Benjamin warns, "The representation of total vitality in life causes fate to end in mad-

---

6   Ibid., 400.

7   Ibid.

ness."[8] In the short aphorism titled "The Great Art of Making Things Seem Closer Together," Benjamin further clarifies this point, arguing that the distance from the near cultivated in the Romantics as well as in the Positivists is itself "ignorance" and praises the traveler who approaches life with "anamnesis" or the capacity to remember (draw near, make relevant and meaningful) events and things from a previous existence. [9] In this sense, nearness *as such* cannot be rejected, but it must also not eclipse that which is distant.

Despite his critiques of nearness, notice that Benjamin is not dismissive of nearness as such. It is rather the mindless conformism or reactivity of that which is *all-too-close* to one's circumstances or the immediacy of events that is the problem. "The less a man is imprisoned in the bonds of fate, the less he is determined by what *lies nearest at hand*, whether it be people or circumstances."[10] Nearness becomes problematic when there is no distance possible from the pressures of what is near at hand. In such circumstances, the individual becomes "imprisoned" by what is too close (the specific stimuli of *these* people at *this* specific moment). Imprisonment of the human being by what is near is precisely what Benjamin describes as stupidity. And on the flipside, when one loses one's self in what is so distant as to be almost unapproachable, then madness ensues.

---

8   Ibid., 396.

9   Benjamin, *Selected Writings, Volume 2*, 247. Although Benjamin does not spell this out in detail, my assumption is that the distance which he speaks of in relation to the Romantics concerns the quasi-transcendental, disinterested distance many of them claimed that ultimately led to their self-isolation. Positivism is likewise given over to the illusion of transcendental autonomy or the God's eye perspective.

10   Benjamin, *Selected Writings, Volume 1*, 398.

That which is distant is, for Benjamin, important precisely because it is the font of human freedom. The free individual is not determined by what is nearest. Rather, the things that determine his/her fate come "from a distance."[11] Imprisonment to what is all-too-close can be contrasted with "prudence toward what is distant" toward which the individual "submits."[12] Too much nearness is equated with imprisonment and stupidity, a narrowing of possibilities down to that which is already configured by a social, political, and economic context. On the other hand, freedom is found in a prudence or careful alertness toward what is most distant from this circumstance.

The stupid or mad individual lacks prudence. The nature of this kind of prudence is further specified at the end of the essay on the psychophysical problem in Benjamin's comments concerning "perfect love" which is a "complete balance between nearness and distance."[13] Benjamin then offers up Dante's Beatrice as an example of perfect love because she is placed amongst the stars (that which is most distant) while at the same time these very same stars are brought close to Dante in and through the individual body of Beatrice. Perfect love is a special kind of bonding between nearness and distance that is characteristic of prudence toward the distant (the intensive, creative, vital powers of nature that fill the corporeal substance with its spirit).

Interestingly, there are definitive political implications for this theory. In another context, Benjamin argues that fascism and capitalism both exhibit a tendency to erase the distant

---

11   Ibid.

12   Ibid.

13   Ibid., 399.

in order to privilege what is near. Benjamin writes that the urban crowd is characterized by a "protective gaze" which "is overburdened with protective functions [...]" to the point that "there is no daydreaming surrender to distance and faraway things."[14] The gaze, emptied of distance, is precisely the mode of looking that characterizes both the flâneur and the National Socialist who are protective of what is near. This connection is made clear when Benjamin writes, "This 'crowd,' in which flâneur takes delight, is just the empty mold with which, seventy years later, the *Volksgemeinschaft* was cast."[15]

In this sense, "constant contact" is a symptom of capitalism's stupidity. It is an attempt to erase what is most distant in order to fixate our attention on what is near at hand. And by doing so, constant contact also threatens our freedom. For teachers, this would mean threatening their freedom to unplug or disengage from students, and for students, this would mean losing the ability to separate themselves from immersion in their social networks. To combat these trends, and to attempt to once again cultivate a balance exhibited by Dante's perfect love for Beatrice, education has to concern itself with understanding what it means to be prudent in the age of digital reproduction.

---

14   Walter Benjamin, *Selected Writings: Volume 4, 1938-1940*, eds. H. Eiland and M. W. Jennings (Cambridge, MA: Belknap Press, 2003) 341.

15   Benjamin, *The Arcades Project*, 345.

CHAPTER 13

Collecting as Posthuman, Antifascist Educational Practice

In this presentation, I want to argue that collecting is a particular kind of educational activity that is shared across species.
In this sense, it has certain posthuman potentialities that have
yet to be completely appreciated in posthumanist literature or
posthumanist educational practice. To argue this point, I will
turn to Walter Benjamin, whose reflections on collecting are a
unique jumping off point for contemplating the connections
between collecting, studying, and other-than-human animals.

In his epic, sprawling, unfinished text that charts the rise
and fall of the arcades in 19th century Paris, Benjamin makes
the following, rather brief and elusive observation, "Collecting
is a primal phenomenon of study: the student collects knowledge."[1] There are several aspects of this citation that are crucial
to point out. First, collecting is a *primal* phenomenon of study.

---

1   Benjamin, *The Arcades Project*, 210.

This means that collecting is *essential* and *foundational* to any theory and practice of study. All studying is a form of collecting (of course this does not always mean that all collecting is studying, e.g., collecting souvenirs). Second, it is important to point out that the collector collects something in particular: Knowledge. But what kind of knowledge is this? While we might tend to think of knowledge in cognitive terms, there are many passages throughout Benjamin's works that suggest how knowledge is first and foremost not about cognitive or mental concepts so much as tactile, embodied, preconscious knowledge of things and environments. Collecting is perhaps most commonly connected up with Benjamin's interest in the flâneur. Yet there is an important distinction that is lost when we collapse the two. In his essay on Fuchs, Benjamin observes, "Romantic figures include the traveler, the flâneur, the gambler, and the virtuoso; the collector is not among them."[2] What is the distinction? In *The Arcades Project* Benjamin argues that "Collectors are beings with tactile instincts. Moreover, with the recent turn away from naturalism, the primacy of the optical that was determinate for the previous century has come to an end [...] The flâneur optical, the collector tactile."[3] Indeed, for Benjamin, the motto of the flâneur is "Look, but don't touch!" The distance afforded by the gaze stands in sharp contrast to the intimate nearness of the collector to his or her objects. Whereas the flâneur emphasizes the eye, the collector emphasizes the hand—one moves out to get a broader view the other moves in close to touch. This point is even more explicit in Benjamin's reflections on unpacking his

2   Benjamin, *Selected Writings, Volume 3*, 275.

3   Benjamin, *The Arcades Project*, 206-7.

COLLECTING AS PRACTICE   119

book collection. There he writes, "As he [the collector] holds them [his books] in his hands, he seems to be seeing through them into their distant past as though inspired."[4] The collector thinks through hands, through the faculty of touch.

In short, the studier collects tactile knowledge of the world, and it is this tactility which positions collecting as a special kind of educational practice poised between human and other-than-human animals. For instance, Benjamin casts "animals (birds, ants), children, and old men as collectors."[5] Collecting, I want to argue, as a studious practice is a diasporic educational form of life that does not necessitate human-centric forms of attentiveness and valuation. Instead, it touches upon the other-than-human within the human.

In the short aphorism titled "Gloves" Benjamin highlights how tactility is a faculty which is between the human and the animal, hence bourgeois aversions to touch (think here of the prioritization of vision for the flâneur). Benjamin writes, "In an aversion to animals, the predominant feeling is fear of being recognized by them through contact. The horror that stirs deep in man is an obscure awareness that something living within him is so akin to the disgust-arousing animal that it might be recognized. All disgust is originally disgust at touching."[6] Touch is the zone of indistinction between the human and the other-than-human animal. Because of this, there is something disgusting about it that must be repressed through

4   Walter Benjamin, *Selected Writings: Volume 2, Part 2, 1931-1934*, eds. M. W. Jennings, H. Eiland, and G. Smith (Cambridge, MA: Belknap Press, 2005), 492.

5   Benjamin, *The Arcades Project*, 211.

6   Benjamin, *Selected Writings, Volume 1, 1913-1926*, 448.

mastery over and against it. If collecting is a practice of study, and it is uniquely connected with touch, then there is also something about the collector that is disgusting, or socially awkward. Indeed, Benjamin argues that there is something in the collector that is "behind the times" and causes "distrust of the collector type."[7] The collector has been contaminated by precisely that which ought to be externalized and mastered: a haptic entanglement with objects.

Children, in particular, study the world through collecting things and gestures and thus are close to the other-than-human world in ways that elude adults. Benjamin's word for this kind of haptic, embodied collecting is mimesis or sensuous mimicry. Through mimicry the child touches the other, and in touching, takes up the gestures of the other as his or her own gestures. Mimicry is a collecting of gestures through their embodied displacement.

For example, Benjamin recounts gazing into the aquarium of an otter in the Berlin Zoological Gardens as a child. He remembers, "when I gazed into the water, it always seemed as though the rain poured down into all the street drains of the city only to end up in this one basin and nourish its inhabitants."[8] The otter would become the "sacred animal of the rainwater." On rainy days, the young Benjamin would sit inside his house and stare out the window. "In good rain," he writes, "I was securely hidden away [...] In such hours passed behind the gray-gloomed window, I was at home with the

---

7   Benjamin, *Selected Writings, Volume 2, Part 2, 1931-1934*, 491.

8   Benjamin, *Selected Writings, Volume 3, 1935-1938*, 366.

otter."[9] Thus, human and other-than-human worlds touch through a series of sensual resemblances, a series of literal and figurative points of touching in which the watery world of the otter and Benjamin's home come to resemble each other despite differences. This does not mean that they coincide (or are reducible to one another), but rather that they overlap in precisely those moments when embodied, mimetic entanglements outrun reasonable distinctions and logical categorizations. In these temporary flashes, the stability of the human "I" that holds experience together gets caught up in sensation in a way that destabilizes the human. Benjamin, as a child, *strays* from the human-centric path, crossing ontological boundaries, mingling with the creaturely through the collection of haptic touchpoints.

Touch is fleeting (not unlike palpitations), and the chiasmic meeting on the human and nonhuman cannot stabilize into a set habit without being turned back into a grasping, a holding, an anchoring in the human. It must always be found in the distracted moment when the self lets go of itself and yields to sensations that are no longer identifiable according to the logic of existing (human) habits and not yet fully formed and sedimented ways of life. In this sense, the contingency of the mimicry is itself a redoubling of the "extremely flighty" pondering of animals.[10] Animal pondering is, in other words, distracted. Benjamin has in mind the various creatures in Kafka's worlds, such as the animal in "The Burrow" who "flits

---

9   Ibid.

10   Benjamin, *Selected Writings, Volume 2, Part 2, 1931-1934*, 810.

from one worry to the next."[11] From a human-centric perspective, one might read this as a criticism, as animals lack the attentiveness of the human. Yet for Kafka, creaturely distraction is precisely what gives animals "the greatest opportunity for reflection." As such the absent-minded, temporary, contingent mimicry of the child is not merely play. There is an educational dimension at work here. Through mimesis, the child sensually studies the outlines of a creaturely life that exceeds definition yet is suddenly made visible (it is made knowable) in the form of a sensuous resemblances. Such creaturely life is not found in existing human or animal habits but rather exists only in a momentary flash wherein bodies touch that which exists between forms of life.

The adult can approximate this mimetic ability through collecting. Here we can give more specificity to the "childlike element" which Benjamin finds in collecting. The collector, like the child, is concerned with the "renewal of existence."[12] Collecting, painting, cutting figures, application of decals are some of the activities which enable children to renew the world. Through "touching things" to "giving them names," children find within the world untapped potentialities.[13] Here I would like to emphasize *touching*. Children have the capacity to renew the world through a haptic engagement with it, which *produces* similarities across differences. We can connect Benjamin's observation concerning renewal, touching, and collecting, with the mimetic relation which children and collectors share in relation to the world of things. Like the child

11   Ibid.

12   Ibid., 487.

13   Ibid., 492.

who hides behind the door only to *become* wooden, ridged, creaky, so too the collector "disappear[s] inside" the collection.[14] The collector (subject) and collection (object) become intimately interwoven. Indeed, it almost ceases to make sense to refer to subjects and objects at all. Rather what appears is a kind of assemblage or *ecology* that is decisively other-than-human, reaching out across the divide that separates organic and inorganic, animate and inanimate divisions. The life of the collector is therefore defined in terms of its entanglements with other-than-human entities. Such entanglements might be "disgusting" yet they are a way of touching upon a future, creaturely potentiality through child-like mimesis which always takes the human to its absolute swelling point.

On this reading, Benjamin's other-than-human turn is a kind of distraction from the human, opening up a studious space and time that is *transversal* or *diasporic*. If Benjamin once argued that the teleology of education *as such* concerns the cultivation and verification of the "complete human being, the citizen" here we have another kind of education.[15] Indeed, we might argue that the apex of education for the "complete human being" is none other than fascist education, which is concerned exclusively with the purity of the Aryan race. As such, fascist education is an education of boundaries and borders, strict ontological distinctions and racialized categorizations (indeed, the Jew was considered "subhuman" because of its proximity to other-than-human lifeforms). For Benjamin, this strange location betwixt and between the human and the other-than-human is as creaturely as it is antifascist. Collect-

14   Ibid., 492.

15   Benjamin, *Selected Writings, Volume 2, Part 1*, 273.

ing as a tactile practice of study enables us to gain access to the creaturely as a potentiality for another kind of life beyond the hard and cold distinctions drawn by fascist education.[16] As such, collecting becomes a feral, posthuman education and the classroom a bestiary of strange creatures that prefer not to become complete human beings.

---

16   See Chapter 7 in this volume for an analysis of fascist hardness and coldness.

PART V

The Aesthetics of Education

CHAPTER 14

RETHINKING CURIOSITY IN
EDUCATIONAL PHILOSOPHY

In this paper, I want to trouble three assumptions about curiosity found in educational philosophy.[1] First, Paulo Freire
argues that curiosity is "epistemological," meaning it concerns
how we think about our lived experience. I would like to suggest that instead of epistemological, curiosity is aesthetic—it
concerns what we can see, feel, taste, touch, and so forth. Second, curiosity is often thought of as a form of attention. It is
some kind of experience that involves focusing on an experience. Yet, I will contend that curiosity is first and foremost
found in moments of distraction, or a pulling away from what
is of primary concern in order to experience the periphery or
the margin. Third, curiosity is often thought of as an active,
willed decision. For instance, if one is curious about some-

---

1   This paper was accepted to the American Educational Research Association Conference in 2019, which was canceled due to
COVID-19.

thing, then one pursues it. Yet, I will argue that the initial sensation of curiosity is not willed at all, but rather is a willingness to passively yield to something that strikes one's perceptual field. This might pose a challenge to the will, but it should not be confused with the will as such. In short, I will call for a new appreciation of the more or less underappreciated aspects of curiosity (including its aesthetic, distracted, and passive aspects) as educationally relevant.

First, in my book titled *The Aesthetics of Education: Theatre, Curiosity, and Politics in the Work of Jacques Rancière and Paulo Freire*,[2] I critically evaluate Freire's highly influential theory of curiosity. For Freire, curiosity is a natural disposition toward the world that enables us to question the fundamental fixity of reality in order to cultivate a critical consciousness. He even refers to curiosity as "epistemological curiosity" or a curiosity that concerns how we think and how we come to uncover and reveal the hidden truths of our historical situation.[3] If schooling practices anesthetize curiosity, Freire's critical pedagogy reawakens it as a crucial factor in education for human liberation.

My problem with Freire's analysis has less to do with the political potential of curiosity for liberation projects and more to do with the firm insistence that curiosity is first and foremost concerned with epistemological questions about what can be consciously known. According to Freire, epistemological curiosity unveils the world, allowing us to "think accurate-

---

2   Lewis, *The Aesthetics of Education*.

3   Paulo Freire, *Pedagogy of the Heart*, trans. D. Macedo and A. Oliveira (London: Continuum, 1997), 100.

ly" about experience from the standpoint of the oppressed.[4] Such thinking is, for Freire, the core of a critical science of lived experience. Indeed, epistemological curiosity, on this view, is decisively separated out from aesthetic questions. This division is, in large part, the result of Freire's desire to maintain the scientific rigor of his largely Marxist approach to historical knowledge. But science also has to be supplemented by an aesthetic dimension in the form of a motivational and inspiring narrative. Thus, curiosity does not "refuse to consider the aesthetic" but rather "avails itself of it."[5] Aesthetics comes *after* curiosity, and curiosity *makes use of* aesthetics. Epistemology is separated from aesthetics, and they are placed in a rather linear trajectory, the latter following the former as a necessary supplement.

There are educational implications to this division of labor between knowing and sensing, but what I would like to emphasize here is the phenomenologically inaccuracies of Freire's description. For instance, curiosity is first and foremost experienced as a snagging of the eye. It is an effect on our sensorial orientation in the world. Some small detail suddenly pops out of the background, becoming relevant to us. According to Jacques Rancière, curiosity "does not know in advance what it sees and thought does not know what it should make of it."[6] In other words, the eye and its grasp of the situation is suddenly undone, and this shift in what can be sensed within

---

4   Paulo Freire, *The Politics of Education*, trans. D. Macedo (Massachusetts: Bergin & Garvey Publishers, 1985), 3.

5   Freire, *Pedagogy of the Heart*, 96.

6   Jacques Rancière, *The Emancipated Spectator*, trans. G. Elliott (London: Verso, 2009), 105.

a situation then opens up to a thought that does not know what to think. Curiosity begins with aesthetic repartitioning of the sensible. For this reason, curiosity does not pierce below the illusions of the knowing subject to penetrate a hidden truth (as in the scientific or epistemological model proposed by Freire). Instead, it merely reorganizes or reorients the field of the visible. It does not know what is behind so much as it feels what is to the side. The thinking that is produced is never free from the contamination of appearances and can never be purely scientific.

Second, curiosity does not concern attentiveness so much as distraction. In educational literature, attentiveness is taken for granted as an assumed educational good. Figures such as Nel Noddings equate attentiveness with an ethic of care, and, more recently, Jan Masschelein and Maartin Simons argue that attentiveness is the defining feature of educational life.[7] In these philosophies, curiosity plays a marginal role, rarely appearing as an educationally relevant idea. It is my contention that this oversight is because curiosity is not strictly a form of attentiveness to the world. Indeed, the oversight of Noddings and others when it comes to curiosity belies an uncomfortable truth about curiosity: that it is in some way associated with distraction and thus educationally suspect. And this is indeed the case, as curiosity from St. Augustine to Martin Heidegger to Bernard Stiegler has been blamed for any number of educational problems, including the tendency to be distracted from

---

7   Nel Noddings, *Caring: A Relational Approach to Ethics and Moral Education* (Berkeley: University of California Press, 2013); Jan Masschelein and Maarten Simons, *In Defense of the School: A Public Issue* (Leuven, Belgium: E-Ducation, Culture, & Society, 2013).

what matters.[8]

Curiosity pulls us away from being on track or on point. The eye is thrown off its proper course and swerves in directions that are potentially disruptive. Think here of the simple example of a student asking a tangential question in class. Such tangents are often initiated by the student saying, "I am just curious..." Just curiosity is a minor deviation, so minor as not to matter. But the cumulative effect of these asides might indicate a larger problem in the project of attention formation in a classroom, as the asides can mount, gaining momentum, and in turn, causing the whole class to become curious about precisely what should not matter.

The distractive quality of curiosity makes it educationally unique and interesting. Stated differently, curiosity enables us to think through the possible educational value of distraction as an opportunity (rather than an obstacle) for opening up new possibilities for seeing and thinking about the world. To be distracted is not a deficit so much as a real educational potentiality to see otherwise. Such a perspective de-pathologizes distraction as an educational illness needing the cure of attentiveness. And politically it proposes that the problem might not be attention deficit disorder so much as what Susan Sontag once called "attention excess disorder" or a tendency to become too attentive so as to miss minor fluctuations in the field of the visible, audible, or sensible that could indicate alternative forms of life beyond the status quo.

8   See Tyson E. Lewis, "The Dude Abides, or Why Curiosity is Important for Education Today," in *Curiosity Studies: A New Ecology of Knowledge*, eds. P. Zurn and A. Shankar (Minneapolis: University of Minnesota Press, 2020) for a more detailed analysis of this philosophical lineage.

In my contribution to the book *Curiosity Studies: A New Ecology of Knowledge* edited by Perry Zurn and Arjun Shankar, I explore this counter-intuitive thesis in relation to the character "The Dude" in the film *The Big Lebowski*. On my reading, the Dude fully embodies a distracted form of life which at first might appear to summarize many of the worries espoused by the critics of curiosity. Yet, if we let the film distract us from our own attention to attentiveness, it actually articulates a form of life that is open to educational experiences on the periphery of consciousness. The Dude solves the crime at the heart of the film not through careful attention to clues (as might be the case with other detectives such as Sherlock Holmes) but rather through a loose, improvisational, drifting, meandering style of being in the world that is characteristic of curiosity's own distracted nature.

This last point about the Dude brings me to my third observation. Curiosity is not about willful attention. As Paul North writes in his book *The Problem of Distraction*, distraction is difficult to describe because the minute that one willfully attempts to be attentive to it, it disappears.[9] In this sense, it can only emerge in the margins of experience or on its periphery as a momentary lapse of the will. Instead of willfully cultivating curiosity, education ought to willingly let curiosity happen—let students yield to it as it emerges. The podcast titled "Choose to be Curious" is therefore problematic. Although I have been featured on this great podcast and have the utmost respect for the host, Lynn Borton, I would like to suggest one can never choose to be curious. One can be affected by curiosity, and can be open to this affect, but one

---

9   North, *The Problem of Distraction*.

cannot choose it. Choosing makes it sound like curiosity can be willed, yet one cannot will to be curious about something, rather one is drawn toward something that seems to interrupt or suspend whatever one was willfully doing.

Instead of conflating curiosity with the will, I propose another formulation. Curiosity happens to us, we yield to it. This yielding can be small, as when a student off the cuff raises a hand and says "I'm just curious about x." Or the yielding can turn into a more sustained approach to a topic. In both cases, curiosity *poses a challenge to the will* either to resist its interruption or to take it up and transform it into an attentive practice. As such, there is no natural or necessary relation between curiosity and attention. Instead, attention can emerge out of a curious distraction if and only if the will takes responsibility for the curious moment, transforming the passive receptivity of curiosity into an active project of willful pursuit.

In conclusion, curiosity needs to be rethought in educational philosophy as an embodied, aesthetic form of distracted yielding to the appearance of an anomalous detail or minor variation in the partitioning of the sensible. As such, it is equal parts annoyance and promise. It is annoying in that it is a kind of aesthetic *dérive* that could cause a lapse in concentration when concentration is most needed. But it might also and equally be a promise that something different can enter into a classroom that is beyond the willful pursuits of the teacher or the students. In the words of the Dude, perhaps the challenge today is to think about what it might mean to allow space and time for abiding in our classrooms.

CHAPTER 15

IMAGE AS IGNORANT SCHOOLMASTER:
A LESSON IN DEMOCRATIC EQUALITY

In this paper, I want to highlight the importance of the aesthetic regime of the arts for Jacques Rancière's theory of the ignorant schoolmaster and emancipatory education. And in making this argument, I will highlight the unique role that a return to the arts can play in democratic education. In this sense, ignorant teaching has its roots in a certain aesthetic revolution. To argue this, I will quickly outline four major dimensions of Rancière's description of the radical 19th century French teacher Joseph Jacotot's pedagogical practice and then compare and contrast these dimensions with the central features of the arts of the aesthetic regime.

To begin, ignorant teaching is composed of the following set of characteristics:

1) Ignorance: Jacotot first experimented with the method of emancipatory teaching when asked by a group of

Flemish students to teach them how to speak French. With no shared language between them, he told them through an interpreter to translate a French text of a bilingual edition of *Télémaque*. Surprisingly, the students were able to teach themselves French without Jacotot explaining anything. Summarizing, Rancière writes, "The fact was that his students [meaning Jacotot's] had learned to speak and to write in French without the aid of explication."[1] Ignorance, rather than a deficit, becomes a kind of asset to teaching. When a teacher knows something, there is always the temptation to either (a) explicate it to the student or (b) to hide it like Jean-Jacques Rousseau did with Emile. In the first case, stultification sets in and in the second case, teaching becomes an act of deception. Both of these—stultification and deception—produce intellectual subordination. To avoid both of these temptations and thus a reproduction of subordination, Rancière highlights the potentially emancipatory role of ignorance in teaching.

2) Equality of Intelligences: The discovery that the Flemish students could teach themselves French not only disturbed the logic of pedagogical explication and deception. It also suggested that all intelligences are of the same nature. No longer can clear hierarchies between intelligences be firmly established. Instead, a new educational hypothesis was introduced by Jocotot that starts from a position of verifying an equality that is already present rather than producing an equality yet-to-come.

---

1   Rancière, *The Ignorant Schoolmaster*, 9.

3) Pointing: If the teacher does not explicate or deceive, then what role does he or she play? The ignorant schoolmaster introduces a book to be held in common and points to it. The ignorant schoolmaster's essential gesture is thus twofold. First, he or she places something in common and says, "Look at this, it is important." This causes a moment of distraction (from whatever might concern the *individual* students) and then reorientation toward the shared thing that is now held in common. Second, the ignorant schoolmaster then verifies an attempt to manifest the equality of intelligences in relation to the thing held in common. In sum, the ignorant schoolmaster verifies the work of intelligence in relation to a common thing.

4) Authority: But why should the student listen to the ignorant schoolmaster? Here the importance of referring to the teacher as a schoolmaster becomes important. Although ignorant of what he or she teaches, such a schoolmaster nevertheless has a certain authority to demand a willful attempt and verify it. The function of the master is to "command" the will of the student to keep trying, keep looking, keep going.[2] Indeed, instead of explicative statements, the ignorant schoolmaster gives imperatives like "Don't stop!" Thus, the force of the ignorant schoolmaster's will doubles in inverse proportion to his/her knowledge.

These four dimensions are the essential features of ignorant teaching and culminate in a fundamental insight: emancipa-

---

2   Ibid., 13.

tion cannot follow from stultification or deception. Rancière summarizes this as follows: emancipation is "each man becoming conscious of his nature as an intellectual subject."[3] But the origin of these four dimensions of emancipatory teaching lie outside the pedagogical field. Indeed, it is my argument that they are derived from certain aesthetic innovations which began either coterminous with Jocotot's experiments or during the previous century in French letters. This argument is not that unexpected granted Rancière's own insight into the relationship between aesthetics and critical theory. In his book titled *The Aesthetic Unconscious*,[4] Rancière claims that Freudian psychoanalysis was made possible because of certain innovations within the aesthetic regime of the arts. This regime refers to a post-Kantian idealist and romantic aesthetic revolution that troubles hierarchical divisions between art and non-art as well as rankings within art itself concerning the value of certain genres. Further, a prime example of an ignorant schoolmaster offered in the book of the same title is none other than the poet Racine whose work is given as a lesson in the equality of intelligences. As an "emancipated artist"[5] Racine must assume that everyone can think, speak, and read.[6] Thus, the poet embodies the opposite of the "professor's stultifying lesson."[7]

Given this description of the rise of the aesthetic regime as

3   Ibid., 35.

4   Jacques Rancière, *The Aesthetic Unconscious*, trans. D. Keates and J. Swenson (Cambridge: Polity Press, 2009).

5   Rancière, *Ignorant Schoolmaster*, 70.

6   Ibid.

7   Ibid.

well as the primacy of poetics in Rancière's theory of emancipation, we can now return to our four essential dimensions of ignorant teaching, but with an aesthetic twist:

1) Ignorance: It might at first appear that art knows too much. Indeed, Rancière refers to the key role of the "intelligence of the book" used by Jacotot in his initial experiments in equality.[8] Rancière also refers to the "pensiveness" of images.[9] But it is important to point out that just because something has intelligence and is thoughtful does not mean that it knows something, least of all what it itself is or does. Agreeing with this point, Rancière states that pensive images think, but this thinking is decisively "indeterminate."[10] Further it is a thinking that does not take place behind the field of representation but on the surface, in the mixing of various regimes of expression (such as romanticism and neoclassicism). Such a play between forms, genres, and styles enables images to remain pensive while also decisively indeterminate. Such imagistic indeterminacy is the thought proper to art of the aesthetic regime.

2) Equality: As has already been alluded to, arts of the aesthetic regime offer *resistance* to any notion of fixed, hierarchically ordered boundaries and thus embody *equality*.[11] No longer are certain things "off limits"—rocks and

---

8   Ibid, 13.

9   Rancière, *Emancipated Spectator*, 122.

10   Ibid, 108.

11   For a more detailed analysis of the aesthetic regime of the arts,

washerwomen, urban detritus and crass commercial advertisement, toothpicks and comets are all equally possible subjects for artistic representation. As such, there is something radically democratic about the pensiveness of images. Suddenly everything thinks and needs deciphering—even the smallest, most "insignificant" details of everyday life become hieroglyphics. While such meaning exists in excess, the pensiveness of these variegated texts and images testifies to the recalcitrant nature of texts to show their hand (so to say). In other words, the expressivity of a text is ambiguous and indeterminate, and in this dialectic, reveals that no one absolute meaning is possible, no conclusive interpretations can be drawn, that no intention can possibly control where, when, and how texts will be taken up. Pensiveness guarantees that no description is exhaustive or perfect, that there is no seamless and continuous connection between words, things, and actions, thus challenging any claim to mastery over such wild texts. Another maxim that is helpful from Rancière is that "everything is in everything."[12] Starting from any point, you can lead yourself to any other point, precisely because of the horizontality of relations established through the aesthetic regime of the arts. All subjects are equally interrelated and interwoven.

3)   Pointing: Because of the pensive indeterminateness of images, they have the potential to wrench us from our habits, throw us offline, distract us, and redirect attention.

---

see Rancière, *The Politics of Aesthetics.*

12   Rancière, *Ignorant Schoolmaster*, 41.

Rancière focuses on how certain kinds of images and imagery lead to "indeterminate effects" that "blur the false obviousness of strategic schemata; they are dispositions of the body and the mind where the eye does not know in advance what it sees and thought does not know what it should make of it."[13] Instead of establishing a link between representations, knowledge of what is represented, and action, pointing to the indeterminate breaks apart these linkages, freezing us in place while we ponder that which arrests our gaze.

4) Authority: Art of the aesthetic regime thinks but has no knowledge of its thoughts. It therefore cannot guide us from image, to knowledge, to action. For this reason, one might think that art loses its authority. Yet for the arts of the aesthetic regime, this is not the case. The authority of art comes from its ability to give a command: "Look at this!" By presenting a radical reshuffling of aesthetic conventions and through a radical juxtaposition of elements, such art causes the eye to stumble over itself and the mind to trip over its own assumptions. Such aesthetic experimentation has a certain authority to command the eye of the viewer to stop and look.

In short, the original ignorant schoolmaster is the work of art of the aesthetic regime. Its authority is a model of ignorance that disorients and reorients precisely because of its indeterminateness. Both schoolmaster and pensive image command: "Hey, stop and look at this!" And this command

---

13   Rancière, *Emancipated Spectator*, 105.

is fundamentally political precisely because the operative logic of the police is: "Keep moving, there is nothing to see here!"[14] The police (as a partitioning of the sensible, or ordering of things, people, roles, and so forth) concerns the flow of traffic (in which everything stays in its proper lane and abides by the speed limit) whereas democratic politics is about the disruptive moment when something or someone appears out of place, when swerves happen within the order of things, people, and roles.

What does this mean for education? While my story is an interesting scholarly comparison, does it offer anything new to educators interested in emancipatory teaching and learning? I would argue that if there is an aesthetic unconscious that makes possible ignorant teaching, then this has two major implications. First, it highlights how ignorant teaching does not merely concern the intellect and the will as Rancière and so many of his commentators have highlighted. Instead, it more fundamentally concerns an aesthetic repartitioning of what can and cannot be seen. Ignorant teaching concerns who *appears* as intelligent or what *appears* as a willful act. Without a sensorial adjustment that shifts the line of vision of the ignorant schoolmaster, then the hypothesis of the equality of intelligences will remain a mental construct rather than a perceptual reality that is verifiable in what is seen or heard (not merely thought). We have to *see* students as capable of their own learning. It is not just enough to think this. Second, my argument might suggest a new primacy for art in democratic

---

14   Tyson E. Lewis, "Move Around! There is Something to See Here: The Biopolitics of the Perceptual Pedagogy of the Arts," *Studies in Art Education* 57, no. 1 (2015): 53-62.

educational discourse. Instead of art being a specialized niche within educational thought, the idea of the image as *the* first and primary ignorant schoolmaster might return us to the studio, or the gallery, or the museum as essential rather than peripheral locations for thinking about teaching and learning. This does not mean that pensive images offer didactic lessons in *how* to teach or *what* to teach. Rather they might offer a more oblique yet fundamental lesson: that anyone and anything *can* teach.[15]

---

15   But this does not mean that art and education are the same. Indeed, there are important differences to point out. In this sense, the arts of the aesthetic regime are a point of departure. One key difference is that the arts do not verify anything. The results of their command remain as indeterminate as their content.

PART VI

Education and Organization

CHAPTER 16

Revolutionary Leadership ↔
Revolutionary Pedagogy:
Re-evaluating the Links and Disjunctures
Between Lukács and Freire

A major problematic in Marxist theory is how to conceptualize, or reconceptualize, revolutionary organization. A
useful topography of the various historical modes of organization is provided by Michael Hardt and Antonio Negri in
their highly controversial and conceptually rich book *Multitude*.[1] Here the authors suggest that any theory of counterhegemonic resistance must be framed by a historical materialist
understanding wherein (a) resistance is always in relation to a
specific form of oppression, (b) resistance is determined in the
last instance by changing forms of economic and social production, and (c) each new form of resistance organization is an

---

1   Michael Hardt and Antonio Negri, *Multitude: War and Democracy in the Age of Empire* (London: Penguin, 2005).

attempt to correct the antidemocratic failures of the previous forms. Thus, we see correspondences between the formation of people's armies and the rise of an industrial working class out of a peasant/feudal system.

While these hierarchically organized armies might very well have been necessary at that historical phase, they had increasingly antidemocratic tendencies that negated their stated goals of liberation. In the nineteen sixties, there was a turn to guerrilla organizations in response to the failures of the "party" and the growing restructuring of productive relations on a global scale. Yet even here, the supposedly democratic and decentralized form of organization led to reterritorialization by the guerrilla leader. Now a new crisis/historical opportunity has opened up calling for a reimagining of revolutionary organization. According to Hardt and Negri, transnational, net-worked production acts as the material precondition for a struggle against "Empire" capable of finally articulating a democratic praxis of revolution. Yet the question of what this network looks like remains vague and, as many have suggested, highly allegorical. So Hardt and Negri open a line of inquiry—pinpointing possible tendencies—rather than offer a solution. It is their urgent framing of the issue rather than their final model that remains most important for current grass-root struggles and political theorists.

The crisis of revolutionary organization is also a central issue in contemporary Marxist educational literature. Peter McLaren's recent work indicates a concerted effort to theorize the international organization of the "educational left" into a viable counterhegemonic revolutionary bloc. Thus, he ponders what form of organization this coalition should take given the realities of transnational capitalism. McLaren writes, "critical educators need a philosophy of organization that sufficiently addresses the dilemma and the challenge of the global proletariat."[2] He then lists important new developments in revolutionary struggles that the educational left might find useful in constructing a plausible model for their own praxis: horizontal and not vertical orchestration, social cooperation via democratic dialogue, and so on. While this list is useful, I would like to argue that if the educational left is to be more than simply another counterhegemonic bloc (and thus comprise more than simply those who are employed as educators), it must realize that within itself there lies an important resource for rethinking the problematic of organization: pedagogy. Marxist theories of revolutionary organization should not simply be imported into the struggles of the nascent educational left. Rather, the educational left itself contains a valuable insight into organization that it can and should export out into broader discussions concerning the direction of revolution today.

This essay is an attempt to reframe debates in Marxism in terms of the question of pedagogy and its relevance to the problem of revolutionary organization. I will focus on the relationship between Georg Lukács and Paulo Freire. It is my contention that Freire picks up on a question which Lukács raises but never adequately answers: that is, the question of communication between revolutionary actors. It is my goal —through an analysis of these two theorists—to move pedagogy into the center of revolutionary theory and revolutionary theory back into the center of the critical pedagogy tradition.

---

2   Peter McLaren, *Capitalists and Conquerors: A Critical Pedagogy Against Empire* (Lanham: Rowman and Littlefield, 2005), 63.

Review of the Problematic

Pedagogy has always been a concern in Marxist thought. In the preface to the French edition of *Capital: Volume One*, Karl Marx himself posed the question of pedagogy. To the French citizens he wrote, "I applaud your idea of publishing the translation of Capital as a serial. In this form the book will be more accessible to the working class, a consideration which to me outweighs everything else."[3] Here Marx enthusiastically endorses the French translators' attempt to answer the question of presentation, a question that is assuredly pedagogical in origin. Yet Marx is also hesitant, and in the following paragraph he demonstrates more reserve:

> The method of analysis which I have employed, and which had not previously been applied to economic subjects, makes the reading of the first chapters rather arduous, and it is to be feared that the French public, always impatient to come to a conclusion, eager to know the connection between the general principles and the immediate questions that have aroused their passions, may be disheartened because they will be unable to move on at once.[4]

Thus, Marx reaches a pedagogical standstill. He emphatically states the need for raising the class-consciousness of the workers, yet at the same time recognizes the difficulties of teaching his own text to the masses. In an overtly Hegelian moment, Marx concludes that the only solution is to teach the workers "not to dread the fatiguing climb" towards the "luminous summits" of the dialectic.[5] As such, the difficult labor of the concept is largely left to the intellectual labor of the

---

3   Karl Marx, *Capital: Volume One* (London: Penguin Classics, 1990), 104.

4   Ibid.

5   Ibid.

workers themselves as part of the historical struggle to attain class consciousness. There is therefore no mediation between the hard labor of the individual and the difficulty of the dialectical conception of capital except the struggle itself. The place of pedagogy remains open yet empty in the preface, and the Marxist pedagogical imagination is left for further explorations. In other words, Marx pinpoints the problem of education yet lacks a pedagogical solution to this problem.[6]

The question concerning Marxian pedagogy reaches its crisis point in the work of Lukács who, more than anyone else in the Marxist tradition (except perhaps for Antonio Gramsci), focused on the issue of organization. Below I will argue that in Lukács's work we clearly see the urgent need in Marxism for a theory of communication between revolutionary leaders and workers. While gesturing towards dialogical pedagogy as the tool for facilitating such communication, Lukács's theory of revolutionary education remained underdeveloped. In this essay, I will argue that Freire's *Pedagogy of the Oppressed* is—in part—a response to Lukács's unfinished yet highly suggestive intonations of a Marxist pedagogical project. Lukács must be read in conjunction with Freire in order to understand how to think through pedagogy from within a revolutionary Marxist framework.

Besides passing reference to Lukács in Freirian scholarship, there has yet to be a serious investigation of the links between the Hungarian Marxist critic and the Brazilian educator. For instance, Paul Taylor argued that Freire acquired his view of

---

6   Ford recently argued Marx solves this problem through his distinction between the methods of inquiry and presentation. See Derek R. Ford, *Encountering Education: Elements for a Marxist Pedagogy* (Madison: Iskra Books, 2022), 17-41.

history from Lukács.[7] Here Freire is presented in terms of a continuity with Lukács, a continuity that in many ways misses the very real disjunctions that appear between both theorists (disjunctions caused by differing historical locations and differing intellectual traditions). Raymond Morrow and Alberto Torres on the other hand have more recently asserted that Freire represents a radical break from Lukács's vision of the vanguard party.[8] Here Freire reacts against Lukács, exchanging vanguardism for dialogical pedagogy. Yet again, this argument misses its mark. In suggesting that Freire rejected Lukács in full, very real continuities are missed, continuities arising from the shared intellectual investigation of political and revolutionary organization. More perplexing still are those who advocate for a revolutionary reading of Freire, yet have failed to recognize the intimate relationship between the Lukácsian problematic of leadership and Freire's pedagogy.[9] Thus what is needed is a dialectical model to understand this relationship. Through a dialectical framework we can argue that the very disjuncture highlighted by Morrow and Torres is in fact the continuity suggested by Taylor. When read closely in conjunction with Lukács, Freire's *Pedagogy of the Oppressed* presents not simply a break from Lukács but rather a serious investigation into the problem that evolves throughout his writings yet remains unconscious. An analysis of this largely forgotten

---

7   Paul Taylor, *The Texts of Paulo Freire* (Buckingham: Open University Press, 1993).

8   Raymond Morrow and Carlos Alberto Torres, *Reading Freire and Habermas* (New York: Teachers College Press, 2002).

9   Peter McLaren, *Che Guevara, Paulo Freire, and the Pedagogy of Revolution* (Lanham: Rowman and Littlefield, 2002).

relationship is necessary on two accounts. First, I will correct dominant misconceptions within the Freirian tradition, and second, I will strongly realign Freire with a Marxist problematic of revolutionary organization. What I must emphasize at the outset is that this essay is not simply an obscure commentary of interest only to those specializing in the narrow field of Freirian praxis. Rather, I hope to issue a challenge to Marxist scholars in general who have yet to realize the full ramifications of Freire's dialogical praxis for historical materialist theory.

LUKÁCS AND REVOLUTIONARY LEADERSHIP

In the essay "Toward a Methodology of the Problem of Organization," Lukács argues that Marxists have ignored a vital issue of revolutionary praxis. Instead of seeing organization as an intrinsic problematic within Marxism, theoreticians have dismissed it as an anti-intellectual pursuit, thus reinstating a classical division between mind and body, theory and practice. Lukács on the other hand saw organization as a mediation point between the two and, as such, a vital component for furthering a revolutionary struggle. Opposed to models of "spontaneous revolution," Lukács realized that organization was vital to overcoming the historical obstacles preventing the subjectivization of class consciousness, which included a divided and fragmented consciousness in the proletariat, an ongoing antagonism between momentary gains and the ultimate goal of liberation, and the general internalization of the reified world. Highlighting the urgency for a theory of organization, Lukács warned that "large sections of the proletariat remain intellectually under the tutelage of the bourgeoisie; even the severest economic crisis fails to shake them in their attitude."

In other words, the relation between the development of the proletarian standpoint and the objective economic laws of capital could not be conceptualized as mechanistically related. Thus, the crisis of the proletariat involved "not only the economic undermining of capitalism but, equally, the ideological transformation of a proletariat that has been reared in capitalist society under the influence of the life-forms of the bourgeoisie."[10]

This subjective crisis demands an organizational solution, which for Lukács meant the formation of a Communist Party. The party, as the highest stage of revolutionary organization, embodied, in Lukács's language, the "conscious collective will" of the proletariat and as such could guide the progress of the revolution. Here the party form offered the mediation point Lukács was searching for. A party exists between the volunteerism of the "group leader" and the "unimportance" of the masses. To sustain this mediation, a party must contain two important elements. First, members must have the highest level of dedication to the revolution. They cannot in any way waver in their discipline and clarity of purpose, and as such, must abandon notions of bourgeois individualism. Second, members must also maintain the correctness of leadership through their sustained relationship to the masses. Rather than become a reified and institutionalized party as in liberal democracies, a revolutionary party has to sustain a concentrated interaction between itself and the proletariat. But what is the nature of this vital link? Lukács argues against two prevalent notions of leadership. On the one hand, a revolutionary party could

---

10   Georg Lukács, *History and Class Consciousness: Studies in Marxist Dialectics* (Cambridge: MIT Press, 1971), 70–81, 304, and 311.

embody the "unconscious" of the masses and thus act on their behalf. Rather than work with the proletariat, such a party would drive the struggle from behind, pulling secret strings and managing behind closed doors. On the other hand, a party could simply "merge entirely with the spontaneous instinctive movement of the masses." Here, leadership no longer leads, abnegating its ability to make critical judgments concerning correct action.[11]

Opposed to either alternative, Lukács argues that the proper relationship between party and proletariat is a "dialectical alliance."[12] Although there might be organizational differentiation separating a revolutionary party and the masses, they are nevertheless conjoined through the objective reality of class-consciousness itself. To ensure that the organized body does not degenerate into a detached cult of personality or regimented institution, Lukács argues with Lenin that it must adhere to the historical necessity brought to fruition within the revolution. Thus, Lukács is able to state with certainty that the Communist Party, composed of dedicated revolutionaries, represents "the tangible embodiment of proletarian class-consciousness."[13] As such, the final role of party politics is to clarify where the "true interests" of the proletariat lie, thereby "making them conscious of the true basis of their hitherto unconscious actions, vague ideology and confused feelings."[14] To make these interests conscious, the vanguard wing of the

11   Ibid., 315 and 322.

12   Ibid., 332.

13   Georg Lukács, *Lenin: A Study on the Unity of His Thought* (Cambridge, Mass.: MIT Press, 1971), 27.

14   Ibid., 35.

Communist Party has to remain "a step in front of the struggling masses" and "show them the way."[15]

Here we reach a crucial step in Lukács's theory of the Communist Party. While the vanguard is to remain "one step ahead" of the hesitating masses, it nevertheless cannot, as stated previously, lose its connection to the proletariat—hence the dialectic of leadership. On the one hand, a vanguard party must distance itself to lead, but on the other hand, it must, according to Lukács, "be so flexible and capable of learning from them [the working class] that it can single out from every manifestation of the masses, however confused, the revolutionary possibilities of which they have themselves remained unconscious." To remain in this critical point of mediation, Lukács turns towards a theory of education through which the vanguard does not impose its tactics onto the masses but instead learns from the masses. As Lukács argues, a truly radical party "must continuously learn from their [the workers'] struggle and their conduct of it." Here the masses teach the leaders, and the leaders in turn lead the masses.[16]

In sum, Lukács sets up a problem of organization—a problem concerning the orientation of a purely praxis-oriented type of thinking unique to historical materialism. He turns towards a theory of the Communist Party as a form emerging from within the necessity of revolution to guide the proletariat and to unite the oppressed masses. Yet a party itself must resist reification or isolation from the revolutionary masses. To sustain the dialectical interrelationship between party members and the struggle, the vanguard must learn from those

15   Ibid.

16   Lukács, *Lenin*, 35.

it represents, thereby adapting to the immediate needs of a particular situation in which crucial decisions must be made. Hence, Lukács gestures towards a theory of revolutionary education in which leaders and masses learn from each other. And yet, this theory remains underdeveloped in his work. What are the specific pedagogical tactics necessary to remain in communication with the proletariat? What are the specific ways in which leaders can gain the trust of those they represent without replicating alienating or exploitive models of social interaction? Without answering these questions, "faith" in the sincerity of the vanguard is the only guarantee that it will not transform into a dictatorship. These are precisely the questions raised by Lukács's more "egalitarian" form of vanguard organization yet left open for further development. It is my thesis that Freire's dialogical pedagogy addresses this void in Lukács's work, providing the educational tools necessary to achieve the praxis-oriented thinking Lukács advocated.[17]

THE TURN TOWARD REVOLUTIONARY PEDAGOGY

What I am suggesting is that Freire did not simply critique Lukács, but rather found within Lukács the opening for developing a pedagogy of the oppressed.[18] In this sense, Freire, as a close reader of Lukács, furthered his project by providing the pedagogical techniques necessitated by, yet lacking in, the

---

17   Ibid., 35, 36.

18   While it might be disconcerting to Marxists that Freire's theory of the oppressed does not focus exclusively on the working class, this shift could be reinterpreted in light of Hardt and Negri's theory of the multitude as an expansive notion capable of articulating working class struggles with third world struggles, feminist struggles, and other forms of anti-oppressive revolutionary formations.

theory of the vanguard. Key here is that the introduction of dialogic pedagogy addresses the problem of the vanguardist position through negation—a negation that does not result in a simple tactical add-on but rather necessitates a total transformation of the theory and practice of organization. This constitutes its truly revolutionary potential.

Agreeing with Lukács (and supplementing his theory with the realities of colonization), Freire argues that the oppressed cannot come to consciousness of the causes of their systemic oppression. Due to an internalization of bourgeois ideology, the potential subjects of revolutionary action are caught in a vicious cycle of identification with the oppressors, and thus remain objects of exploitation. For Freire, "the oppressed, having internalized the image of the oppressor and adopted his guidelines, are fearful of freedom."[19] They remain passive, fatalistically locked into their position, bound to their object status. For Freire, the oppressed cannot simply come to consciousness on their own but instead need an external facilitator in the form of the teacher.

In the final chapter of *Pedagogy of the Oppressed*, Freire clearly outlines how the question of pedagogy evolved from within a debate concerning revolutionary leadership. Although some would like to detach the pedagogy of the oppressed as a method from its connections to leadership (and thus the thorny question of Marxist revolution), Freire himself clearly saw his pedagogy as a tool to be used within revolutionary organization to mediate the various relationships between the oppressed and the leaders of resistance. Separating earlier

---

19   Paulo Freire, *Pedagogy of the Oppressed* (New York: Continuum, 2001), 47.

chapters in *Pedagogy of the Oppressed* on banking education from this final chapter on revolution misses Freire's most important contribution to thinking through the profound political implications of pedagogy, and in particular dialogical pedagogy. Through dialogue, Freire is able to make a critical move away from a vanguard position while still remaining within the problematic of revolutionary leadership inaugurated by Lukács. In Freire's model, leaders have to enter into solidarity with the oppressed in an authentic revolution. This process demands the "sharing" of knowledge through dialogue.[20] Here Freire cites Che Guevara and the early Fidel Castro as two revolutionaries who engaged in authentic revolution through dialogue.

What is authentic revolution? It is a revolution that not only overthrows oppressors but also is revolutionary in its organization. It does not replicate the modes of leadership adopted to maintain or sustain inequalities. These qualities of oppression include conquest, divide and rule, manipulation, and cultural invasion. All these techniques of the oppressor result in a decisively antidialogical form of leadership. It follows that an authentically revolutionary leadership would be dialogical in form and critical in its content. Such dialogue opens the channels of communication between leaders and oppressed, facilitating an exchange of ideas through which trust and mutual commitment are fostered. So central is dialogue for Freire that he writes, "cultural revolution develops the practice of permanent dialogue between leaders and people."[21] Dialogue offers the crucial mediation through which the leader can learn from

---

20   Ibid., 164.

21   Ibid., 160.

the experience of the oppressed, and the oppressed can learn from the critical knowledge of the leader to understand the totality of social relations.[22] Here Freire understands the internal and largely unconscious movement in Lukács's own position. He sees that Lukács, in theorizing the vanguard was, in reality, signaling towards its ultimate transformation. In this light, Freire's comment that "the requirement is seen not in terms of explaining to, but rather dialoguing with the people about their actions" is not so much a critique of Lukács, as Morrow and Torres would have it, but rather a furtherance of Lukács's project despite Lukács—a realization of Lukács's own revolutionary organizational theory via its negation.[23] Hence the charge that Freire himself was nothing more than a vanguard is both right and wrong: right in the sense that Freire's project arrives through an interrogation of the vanguard position and wrong in that such an observation merely collapses dialogical pedagogy into a vulgar notion of leadership.

In short, Freire makes an interesting move away from the traditional Marxist version of vanguardism towards a new language of the witness. In Lukács's model, the leader of the Communist Party was the embodiment of class consciousness, but for Freire, the dialogical leader has become the "humble and courageous witness" that emerges from "cooperation in a shared effort—the liberation of women and men."[24] The witness is in Freire's hands dialectically fused with the teacher,

---

22   Perhaps this dialectical negation opens a space for thinking of education within politics that does not result in the totalitarianism that Hannah Arendt feared. See Arendt, *Between Past and Future*.

23   Freire, *Pedagogy of the Oppressed*, 53.

24   Ibid., 53.

becoming simultaneously one who records the experiences of others as well as one who actively intervenes into the very processes which silence, marginalize, and exploit the oppressed by creating spaces where their voices can be heard. Unlike the leader who stands in for the implicit consciousness of the proletariat, the witness conceives the other as subject and recognizes this subjectivity without owning it or dictating to it.[25] Emphasizing a latent strain in Lukács's writings, Freire asserts "the leaders cannot say their word alone; they must say it with the people and resist anti-dialogic manipulation or institutional rigidification."[26] For Freire, dialogue thus emerges as not simply a practical tool but as an important theoretical category for understanding what it means to enter into revolutionary organization.

In conclusion, Freire recounts an example worthy of quoting in full. In a given situation, the aspirations of the oppressed end with the singular or particular demand to increase wages. Here the pedagogue is faced with a central dilemma: external invasion by imposing his or her vision for revolution onto the peasant workers or acquiesce to the demands of the oppressed. In a dialectical maneuver recalling Lukács's own theory of party politics, Freire argues this is in fact a false choice and that the real revolutionary leader would engage in a dialogical pedagogy to articulate both positions. We thus have Freire's solution: The leaders must on the one hand identify with the people's demand for higher salaries, while on the other they

25   See Michalinos Zembylas, "Witnessing in the Classroom: The Ethics and Politics of Affect," *Educational Theory* 56, no. 3 (2006): 305–324.

26   Freire, *Pedagogy of the Oppressed*, 178.

must pose the meaning of that very demand as a problem. By doing this, the leaders pose as a problem a real, concrete, historical situation of which the salary demand is one dimension. It will thereby become clear that salary demands alone cannot comprise a definitive solution. The essence of this solution can be found in the previously cited statement by bishops of the Third World that "if the workers do not somehow come to be owners of their own labor, all structural reforms will be ineffective [...] they [must] be owners, not sellers, of their labor [...] [for] any purchase or sale of labor is a type of slavery."[27]

Through dialogue, totality is conceptualized. Dialogue as a strategy for consciousness-raising not only poses reality as a problem to be solved but also leads to critical self-reflection concerning the goals and aspirations of the oppressed. As such, dialogue is the pedagogical model of communication in an authentic revolution, cultivating consciousness raising with the oppressed as a collective subject of history. Lukács's "imputed consciousness" becomes a consciousness that arises from within the productive activity of the oppressed: the activity of education (acting as teachers and students). No longer is this education simply left to historical chance (volunteerism) or to imputation (vanguardism). Rather it emerges from a shared practice of dialogue in which leadership locates teaching as witnessing and witnessing as learning.

Conclusion

In sum, Freire's intervention is a rupture that distinguishes him from Lukács and yet furthers Lukács's organizational theory of revolution by centering dialogical pedagogy as a neces-

---

27   Ibid., 183.

sary tactic of mediation between leadership and the oppressed. What must be emphasized here is that pedagogy is not a mere refinement of a gap in Lukács's thinking (how to open up communication between leadership and the masses), but rather, Freire's insistence on dialogue ends up transforming the structure of organization in its totality. By taking up Lukács's project, Freire must move beyond Lukács, supplanting the vanguard model of leadership with the dialogical model of the teacher as witness whose mission it is to work alongside of and learn from the oppressed while also providing critical perspectives on this development. As such, the "break" with Lukács is in reality a dialectical negation. In conclusion, pedagogy issues a profound challenge to Marxist organizational strategy and, as Lukács would argue, such a challenge strikes at the heart of Marxist theory. While Freire was able to transform our understanding of revolutionary organization, it remains for Marxist scholars to theorize how this shift in practice demands a rethinking of the theory itself. Thus, I return to my opening comment: If the educational left is to move the revolution forward in terms beyond simply numbers, it must make its theoretical intervention into broader debates.

I offer one final comment. If Lukács can be read as a critical rethinking of vanguardism and Freire as the dialectical realization of this critical rethinking in terms of a viable revolutionary praxis, then vanguardism exists within the very concept of critical pedagogy as a negation. The figure of the vanguard (and its "imputed" attribute) haunts critical pedagogy as part of its unconscious. To examine the relationship of Lukács and Freire is thus not simply a clarion call to political theorists to take education seriously, but in the end, it is also a warning to those who argue for a pedagogy of the oppressed: beware of history for, as we all know, the unconscious always returns as a symptom.

CHAPTER 17

Exopedagogical Organization

Exopedagogy is an exodus, but it is not a destruction or negation of the existing set of concepts defining education.[1] Instead, it locates these concepts out of bounds of their traditional locations, usages, and meanings. It struggles over redefining the old language of education in order to experiment with new locations, usages, and meanings that are emergent from within the multitude itself. Just as Michael Hardt and Antonio Negri rethink concepts such as democracy and entrepreneurism, I feel that basic terms such as school, curriculum, and teacher should not be abandoned (and thus left to be appropriated by neoliberals and progressives) but can be reclaimed and infused with the spirit of the commons. They are, in other words, a way to organize an exopedagogical philosophy of exodus from within yet against the current moment.

---

1   This is an undelivered paper written to celebrate the 20-year anniversary of *Empire* by Michael Hardt and Antonio Negri, 2020.

Much like Hardt and Negri's theory of "political realism,"[2] I want to call this approach "educational realism." Below I will outline what school, teaching, and curriculum might look like for an exopedagogy of the multitude.

The first is the *school*. A key argument for Hardt and Negri is that capitalist expropriation is no longer restricted to the factory. Drawing on Marx's original theory of capitalist expansion during the industrial era, Hardt and Negri focus on a shift from formal to "real subsumption"[3] of social relations by capitalism. Whereas the former emphasizes expansion of capitalism, the latter emphasizes intensification of its disciplinary forms of control. No longer is there an outside to capitalism needing to be colonized. Instead, social relations, communication systems, information networks, and affective modes of labor are all subsumed within capitalism. Social life as a whole becomes "immaterial labor"[4] for capitalist expropriation. Capitalism now operates through biopower, or a power that concerns the management of habits, affects, and social relationships as such. This notion of power undermines the classic Marxian distinction between the base and the superstructure, as the superstructure (culture, politics, and the social broadly conceptualized) is now central to economic production (rather than a mere ancillary reflection). The corollary of this thesis is that the industrial proletariat can no longer be *the* central and sovereign motor driving revolution, hence the centrality of the multitude. The working class cannot, in other words,

---

2   Michael Hardt and Antonio Negri, *Assembly* (Cambridge, MA: Harvard University Press, 2017).

3   Hardt and Negri. *Empire*, 255.

4   Ibid., 258.

be a stand-in for all other political movements and political concerns. The agents of revolution pluralize and multiply, but more interestingly, the locations of revolution *out of bounds* of the factory are potentially infinite. Or, perhaps more aptly, society itself has become a factory exploiting the immaterial labor of an underpaid and/or unpaid multitude of "employees." If Marx's problem was *when* the proletariat would revolt, for Hardt and Negri, it is more a question of *where*.

The multitude of political actors are continually subsumed under forms of subjectivity resulting from the command and capture of Empire. These subjectivities include the indebted, the mediatized, and securitized, and the represented.[5] I agree with this list, but I find a major oversight in Hardt and Negri's work in this regard: the subjectivity of the life-long learner. This is a subjectivity that is (a) continually indebted to institutions, (b) continually under threat of economic obsolescence, and (c) forced to become entrepreneurial by seeking out new skills needed to be seen as productive and efficient. If social life has become a factory for producing certain forms of subjectivity desirable to capitalist command and control, then so too has this very same social life become a *schoolhouse* full of entrepreneurial learners faced with the task of searching out learning opportunities to develop the skills and dispositions that are deemed desirable by a fast-passed knowledge economy. Schooling is no longer restricted to the school; it expands outward until the world itself becomes the school. Learning and laboring thus emerge *together* as simultaneously mutually reinforcing discourses and practices—learning economies and

---

5   Michael Hardt and Antonio Negri, *Declaration* (New York, NY: Argo Navis, 2012).

immaterial economies of affect, information, and knowledge can no longer be separated.

We might argue further that learning is the precise way in which biopower manages the education of the multitude, ensuring a form of debt that cannot be paid off and a form of austerity that attempts to restrict the creative and experimental forces of the multitude. But here it is important to highlight another key aspect of Hardt and Negri's general argument: that forms of Power (from above) are always a *reaction to* powers (from below). Resistance comes first. Indeed, Power is a *response* to pressures exerted on it from a multitude of actors. Power exists parasitically off the powers of the multitude to produce the commonwealth. Summarizing this point, Hardt and Negri state, "Revolt [of the multitude] as an exercise of freedom not only precedes but also prefigures the forms that Power will take in reaction."[6] If this is indeed the case, the discourses and practices of the learning society are themselves *responses* to an insurgent educational logic that defies such management. The social schoolhouse of life-long learning is therefore *not ontologically primary* but is a secondary response to the schoolhouse of the multitude. This is a school that is diasporic, creative, and experimental. It can be found anywhere and anytime there is *free time*.

Those in educational philosophy that are currently struggling to reclaim the Greek meaning of *scholé* as free time are correct in highlighting this as *the* educational question that needs to be faced in the present moment.[7] Free time is a time

---

6   Michael Hardt and Antonio Negri, *Commonwealth* (Cambridge, MA: Harvard University Press, 2009), 234-235.

7   Masschelein and Simons, *In Defense of the School*.

of exodus from the productive logic of capitalist learning, and as such, is a precious time for cultivating certain forms of attention-distraction, study, and learning that do not merely reproduce the subjectivities needed by the learning society. Yet, these same educational philosophers are still locked within a traditional notion of the school as a specific location with a specific form composed of specific elements. As such, they miss an opportunity to think of school as socially dispersed, diasporic, urban, and emergent. *Scholé* as part of the educational grammar of the multitude would not be an institutional site so much as a moment of suspension of use that can happen anywhere with anyone.

The second is *teaching*. The goal of political theory today is to conduct co-research with political movements, to help theorize tendencies in the present that can be seized upon. One such tendency is the end of sovereignty within movements. This is not a rejection of leadership per se, but rather a rethinking of leadership outside of verticality and centrality with regards to movements. For instance, Hardt and Negri invert the relationship between strategy and tactics in relation to leadership. Traditionally, leaders were responsible for long-term political strategy while the masses were responsible for moment to moment tactical adjustments. Emerging from within contemporary political movements is an inversion of this order: "*strategy to the movements and tactics to leadership.*"[8] On this model, the multitude is responsible for the long-term goals of political movements while leaders are called on to confront local problems and make immediate decisions in light of the demands of the multitude. This new relation

---

8   Hardt and Negri, *Assembly*, 18.

between leaders and movements resists leadership becoming centralized, and as such, challenges the Power of sovereignty (as the exclusive right to exercise political authority) over the multitude.

Perhaps we can say the same for the figure of the teacher? The challenge here—as articulated by a host of critical and progressive educators—is how to think the figure of the teacher beyond sovereignty. This would amount to a figure of the teacher who is not vertically dominant over students and is not central to the curricular organization of collective, shared learning and studying (in common). The suggested model does not restrict the role of the teacher but rather pluralizes and disseminates it—while also decentralizing it. As progressives such as Dewey suggest, the teacher might, at times, act as a guide. While at other times, lectures might very well be called for. And, at other moments—moments of study in the "undercommons"[9]—no teacher at all is needed, only a collective of fugitive studiers. In all cases, teachers are not there providing strategy for education—securing the ends toward which all education is progressing. Here, the multitude itself is determining how and whether or not means and ends meet up. Teachers are used tactically, meaning locally and contextually, to choreograph learning and/or studying. They are, in this sense, without institutional home, and without professional status. Teachers are, in this sense, radically poor.

Perhaps it is thus time to return to the word pedagogue and its original meaning in Greek. There we find the figure of the *paidagogos* or the old slave who would walk a child from the home to the school. These slaves were usually of foreign

---

9   Harney and Moton, *The Undercommons*.

birth, speaking barbarian Greek. Interestingly, visual images of the pedagogue bear some resemblance to an old, disgruntled Socrates whose physical conditions were unfit for more demanding tasks. Indeed, according to certain accounts, pedagogues were often those too old to work, and thus had little utility for the household economy.[1] They were expected to follow the child everywhere, not only accompanying the child to school but also during meals, exercise at the gymnasium, bathing, and even lectures (where the pedagogues themselves sometimes gained an education). This constant attendance often led to friendship between the pedagogue and his charge, and while there are often criticisms of pedagogues in various memoirs and philosophical treatises, there are also many accounts that give praise to these constant companions.

I do not want to preserve the exact function of the *paidagogos* in ancient Greek and Roman cultures, but what I would like to emphasize is his exopedagogical location between two institutions: the home and the school. He remains in the commons, a transitory figure that helps navigate the contaminated zone that exists between the "safe" and "orderly" economies of the home and the strict discipline and rituals of the school. As a foreigner and a "useless" slave without work, the pedagogue was a liminal, poor figure—part of the count that did not count, or the multitude. One could only be a pedagogue if one did not have a vocation. As Giorgio Agamben might argue, he is a figure of "use." For Agamben, use is neither a *poiesis* (the production of an object) nor a *praxis* (an acting) nor a

---

1   Norman H. Young, "Paidagogos: The Social Setting of a Pauline Metaphor," *Novum Testamentum* 29, no. 2 (1987): 150-176.

labor (as in modern capitalism).[2] A *poiesis* locates its ends in a finished product, yet Greek notions of slavery focused on the use of the slave's body rather than on a result. The "use" of the slave, on Aristotle's account, is akin to the use of seeing, whose result is sight rather than a specific thing seen. The slave was without a work (*ergon*), and was, in this sense, unproductive to the economy of the household. The pedagogue can be thought of as the *paradigm* of slavery in general precisely because he was a figure who was without work in a double sense: he was a useless slave whose only work was without work. But this does not mean that we should agree with contemporary educational philosophers who argue that the teacher's "work" should be seen as a *praxis* or a form of acting. For these thinkers, contemporary forms of learning force the teacher to produce evidence of student learning as if teaching were indeed the making of a product. Here, quantified learning outcomes are the evidence of the "work" of teaching. But this emphasis on student learning as a product of teaching actually distorts the good life of teaching, which some refer to as a *praxis*.

Praxis, unlike *poiesis*, is an end in itself. The end of an action is a virtuous life, a *bios*. Yet, on Agamben's interpretation, a slave's use of the body does not belong to the sphere of *praxis*. The actions of a slave cannot be considered from the point of view of virtue (*aretè*). Like an instrument, the slave's body is not virtuous in itself, and thus cannot be thought of in relation to acting well or badly. If this is the case, then the "teaching" of the pedagogue does not fit into the model proposed today of the "good life" of the teacher as exemplifying virtuous judgment. Alternatively, it might seem that the only way to

---

2   Agamben. *The Use of Bodies.*

thus describe the life of the pedagogue is in accordance with modern conceptions of labor. Yet even here Agamben argues that such an understanding would be an anachronism. Labor, as we think of it today, is abstracted from use. Through mediation of the market, all labor congeals into a single substance (labor power). Yet in ancient Greece, there was no such thing as labor in the abstract. Instead, there were only a plurality of trades, each defining a particular type of activity and unique type of work. Oddly, not only did the pedagogue lack a labor, but he also lacked a trade, as pedagogy was not a trade so much as that which one performed when one's trade became inoperative. Thus, returning to the pedagogue would mean disaggregating teaching from the labor market, emphasizing its concrete specificity. In sum, Agamben argues, "it is possible that the 'use of the body' and the absence of work of the slave are something more or at any rate, different from a labor activity and that they instead preserve the memory or evoke the paradigm of a human activity that is reducible neither to labor, nor to production, nor to praxis."[3]

While contemporary teaching as a professional identity linked to schools is characterized as either (a) work, (b) action, or (c) labor, returning to the pedagogue of ancient Greece enables us to reimagine the life of the teacher as one of use. This is a *tactical* notion of use. The pedagogue is a teacher as *part* of the commons—a shepherd of the commons, or instrument of the commons, or a common body-in-use. The life of the pedagogue is a life of thresholds between institutions, and thus exists in the commons. Indeed, if the commons itself has become a school of the multitude, then the peripheral non-work

3   Ibid., 20.

of the pedagogue can be reclaimed as a central form of life constituting exopedagogical practice and theory.

The third is *curriculum*. A common curriculum is not about producing the commons *per se* but rather about introducing children to the commons or cultivating the powers of commoning: constituent powers. In juridical theory, constituent power is often thought of as an inaugural event that punctures the legal order. Instead of reinstating a juridical notion of constituent power from above, Hardt and Negri opt to rethink the concept from below, from within political struggles of the multitude. From below, constituent power takes on a much more complicated set of characteristics. Rather than a monolithic power, what we see today is the *pluralization* of constituent powers that resist leadership and centralization and a *temporal extension* of these powers into a continual process of open-ended, experimental, democratic collaboration. Hardt and Negri summarize, "In short, the temporal and social unities of constituent power have become plural: the imagined punctual event has extended to a continuous process and the fantasy of a unified people has been expanded to a vast multitude."[4] The problem here is how to prevent constituent powers from simply toppling over into new forms of constituted power existing within rigid, hierarchically organized, juridical systems of rule.

Although Hardt and Negri fail to make this connection, I would offer up an educational solution: exopedagogy can cultivate the capacities of constituent power through a common curriculum. The multitude needs such a curriculum so that constituent powers do not become constituted as cen-

---

4   Hardt and Negri, *Assembly*, 35.

tralized, hierarchically organized Power. It is important here to remember the etymological root of curriculum is *currere* or "to run" or "to run a course." As such, curriculum is not so much a fixed structure to be followed as a dynamic action that is lived. It is a course of life, or courses with life as the life unfolds. Curriculum is *already* a power, the power to run, and it is the *organization* of this power so that one can run a course of life. Thus, it is inherently plural (as life takes many forms) and involves a necessary temporal extension and organization of powers into a course. In short, curriculum emerges from within the course of life that one runs, and as such, is *the educational logic of constituent power.*

The athleticism implied by running a course should be apparent in this meaning of curriculum. To run a course, one needs embodied skills, dispositions, and habits that cultivate constituent powers to (a) run and (b) extend and intensify this running into a course of life. But for my purposes, I would like to emphasize the *artistic* dimension of curriculum, and in particular transform running into *dancing.*[5] On this reading, we can think of curriculum as the choreography of dancing bodies, artfully collaborating in a swarm, cultivating an aesthetic and embodied intelligence. Instead of a series of lesson plans, curriculum as choreography would be a more experimental course for seeing what bodies are capable of when their constitutive powers are pooled together, syncopated. Perhaps we can even coin a new term: *choriculum.*

---

5   Tyson E. Lewis and Steve Valk, "Educational Realism: Defining Exopedagogy as the Choreography of Swarm Intelligence," *Educational Philosophy and Theory* 54, no. 7 (2022): 906-915.

AFTERWORD

Wandering Down Rabbit Holes

Noni Brynjolson

One of the most powerful themes that comes out of this collection is that of studying. For Tyson E. Lewis, studying is decidedly not goal-oriented. It is different from what we typically think of as learning: meeting objectives, making progress, checking off boxes—a means to an end. For Lewis, studying is a way of embracing the means in and of themselves. He writes that as one studies, "there is a constant sense of wondering in the potentiality of thought." As an art historian who teaches undergraduate students, these words reverberated with me. They reminded me of what I love most about teaching: sparking a sense of wonder and curiosity. I was also reminded of what I find frustrating about working within the neoliberal structure of the university: distraction, in the form of wondering and wandering aimlessly, is considered to be a counter-productive habit to avoid or overcome. Lewis's writing, then, helps us see why embracing distraction can be such an important part of conceptualizing a non-economistic education.

So how can educators work within the current educational system to encourage distraction, and disorientation, and getting lost, and being okay with not knowing the answer? As Lewis points out, one of the most common pedagogical models is that of revelation and enlightenment—moving from the shadows triumphantly into the light. Instead, he suggests remaining in the shadows. He writes that returning to the same texts over and over again is one way to resist models associated with development and progress in which learning is instrumentalized. Another way to do this is to wander down rabbit holes. This is something I encourage my students to do, perhaps because it seems particularly well-suited to art history. As a form of studying, it involves giving up goals, giving in to chance, and finding joy in making strange discoveries.

Although this is typically done on one's computer or phone now, there are parallels with other examples throughout history that share the same spirit, and that could be viewed as part of an alternative history of studying. Surrealist games associated with chance were designed as a way to give up conscious control when writing or making art. The best known of these was exquisite corpse, which involved drawing something, folding up part of the paper, and passing it on to the next person to build on, creating a nonsensical or monstrous image. For the Surrealists, games like this were a way of responding not only to the desire to access the unconscious, but as a way of resisting the aims of enlightenment reason more broadly. WWI had recently ended, and many artists were questioning the foundations upon which western society was constructed, and the ways in which capitalism and imperialism had led to such horrific destruction. Creating strange monsters together may seem like a form of light-hearted escapism, but it can also be seen as a form of resistance to these systems. The Situationists would take inspiration from these approaches several decades later with the dérive, which was intended to open up the space of the modern city to non-capitalist uses. As Guy Debord writes, "one or more persons during a certain period drop their relations, their work and leisure activities, and all their other usual motives for movement and action, and let themselves be drawn by the attractions of the terrain and the encounters they find there."[1] Similar to the exquisite corpse game, there is no goal, destination, or endpoint, just endless, distracted wandering. Drawing together, drifting through the city, wandering through a library, or going down an internet rabbit hole are all activities that have no immediate use value, which is part of why they are pleasurable. Activities like this can open up new senses and make us more conscious of our own rituals and patterns of thought, pointing to the inherent aesthetic value associated with the kind of studying that Lewis is interested in.

The phrase 'going down a rabbit hole' originally came from Lewis Carroll, who wrote about Alice falling down a rabbit hole—although her fall is more of a slow drift downwards. While drifting, she encounters cupboards and bookshelves, wonders if she's falling through the center of the earth, ponders whether cats eat bats or bats eat cats, and almost falls

---

1   Guy Debord, "Theory of the Dérive," in *Situationist International Anthology*, ed. & trans. K. Knabb (Berkeley: Bureau of Public Secrets, 1958/1989), 50.

asleep. Then she enters a strange subterranean world filled with bizarre characters and adventures, which seems to parallel the space of the dérive and the Surrealist game—the usual rules do not apply. Going down the rabbit hole meant giving into chance and mystery, and encountering these moments as meaningful in and of themselves, as a kind of study. It is no surprise that *Alice's Adventures in Wonderland* became an inspiration for the psychedelic culture of the 1960s, when the rabbit hole turned into a metaphor for a drug trip, and 'turn on, tune in, drop out' became a common refrain.

The term, more recently, has been used to refer to the distracting nature of the internet and the ease with which we can lose ourselves in searching for something, or go on tangents, or find out extremely specific information about something, drifting and wandering from topic to topic as we open infinite tabs. New paths are created between topics, like desire lines on a map, and an endpoint is very rarely reached. There is always more to find out. As an art historian, the terrain I cover when studying is filled with rabbit holes: reading about Lascaux cave paintings leads to recent (and much older) discoveries in Indonesia, then warty pigs, and what exactly ochre is made out of, neanderthal aesthetics, ancient body art, Cheddar Man, aurochs, the fertile crescent, the history of glass making, faience, Senet, the *Book of the Dead,* sarcophagi, Egyptomania, Victorian mummy unwrapping parties, mummy medicine, mummy brown, Thomas "Mummy" Pettigrew, bog bodies, Tollund Man, Haraldskær Woman, Haraldskær Woman's last meal… the list could continue on and on. The details are interesting, but so is the process of getting lost in the details, making connections, and then sharing them with others. I hope that in modeling this approach to my students they might decide to find their own rabbit holes to wander down.

There is a problem with distracted studying on the internet, however, which is that many of the sites we visit are designed to capture and monetize our distraction. Getting lost can lead to taking the clickbait or feeding the algorithm. Similarly, distraction can feel alienating and isolating in the classroom, especially in the goal-driven atmosphere of the university. How do we encourage "productive distraction" then, which for Walter Benjamin, allowed for a kind of awakening? As Lewis points out, this is a specific kind of disorientation that allows for "an opening up of the body to extended and intensified perceptual capacities."

The potential for this can sometimes lie in numbers, and in making connections with others, maybe by discovering that your rabbit hole connects with someone else's. This might lead to a deeper underground network. Actual rabbit holes are quite shallow and simple, and designed for pure functionality: sleeping, giving birth, hiding from predators. Warrens, on the other hand, are labyrinthine tunnels that connect multiple families and generations. There is a lot that can be taken from this metaphor, especially the notion of experiencing a new reality underground. Lewis connects this kind of studying to the notion of the undercommons discussed by Fred Moten and Stefano Harney, and I see the potential here for a kind of distracted studying that goes beyond dropping out. Debord, too, pointed out that a dérive was best experienced with others. Ideally, he writes, "several small groups of two or three people," who wander aimlessly together. A similar idea is embedded in Lewis's reconceptualization of educational models.

For example, he writes about rethinking curriculum as a kind of choreography: "an unproductive practice that is disinterested in predetermined ends." Instead of lesson plans, this would be an experiment in "seeing what bodies are capable of when their constitutive powers are pooled together, syncopated." Wandering down rabbit holes means being okay with darkness, blindness, shadows, and potentially, making connections with others. It might lead to the pleasure of interconnectedness: one tunnel leads to the next, and the more time we spend wandering through them, the more we become familiar with how they intersect.

I think about one student who gets lost in her sketchbook and works on a never-ending saga about the underworld. Continuing work on this—her own form of studying—means not transforming into a productive citizen and molding herself into the current system. My hope is that through productive distraction, wandering down a rabbit hole might lead students on their own journey underground. This can be difficult, since education in the neoliberal university emphasizes efficiency: we are taught to connect what we are doing to the language of progress, goals, enlightenment, discovery. This is the paradoxical element of trying to conceptualize a Marxist-influenced education within the current system. As these essays make clear, critique is essential, but so is the process of inventing alternatives. Wandering down rabbit holes is essential for this: blindness becomes an asset, and underground networks can become spaces of wonder to explore together.

BIBLIOGRAPHY

Adorno, Theodor. *Aesthetic Theory*. Trans. R. Hullot-Kentor. Minneapolis: University of Minnesota Press, 1998.

Adorno, Theodor. *Critical Models: Interventions and Catchwords*. Trans. H. Pickford. New York: Columbia University Press, 2005.

Agamben, Giorgio. *Homo Sacer: Sovereign Power and Bare Life*. Trans. D. Heller-Roazen. Stanford: Stanford University Press, 1998.

Agamben, Giorgio. *Idea of Prose*. Trans. M. Sullivan and S. Whitsitt. New York: SUNY Press, 1995.

Agamben, Giorgio. *Infancy and History: On the Destruction of Experience*. Trans. L. Heron. London: Verso, 2007.

Agamben, Giorgio. *Nudities*. Trans.. A. Kotsko. Stanford: Stanford University Press, 2009.

Agamben, Giorgio. *Opus Dei: An Archeology of Duty*. Trans. A. Kotsko. Stanford: University of Stanford Press, 2013.

Agamben, Giorgio. *Potentialities*. Trans. D. Heller-Roazen. Stanford: Stanford University Press, 1999.

Agamben, Giorgio. *The Coming Community*. Trans. M. Hardt. Minneapolis: University of Minnesota Press, 1993.

Agamben, Giorgio. *The Time That Remains: A Commentary on the Letter to the Romans.* Trans. P. Dailey. Stanford, Stanford University Press, 2005.

Agamben, Giorgio. *Use of Bodies.* Trans. A. Kotsko. Stanford: Stanford University Press, 2016.

Althusser, Louis. *Lenin and Philosophy and Other Essays.* Trans. B. Brewster. New York: Monthly Review Press, 1971/2001.

Althusser, Louis. *Philosophy for Non-Philosophers.* Trans. G.M. Goshgarian. London: Bloomsbury, 2014/2017.

Althusser, Louis. *Philosophy of the Encounter: Later Writings, 1978-1987.* Trans. G.M. Goshgarian. New York: Verso, 1993/2006.

Althusser, Louis. *The Humanist Controversy and Other Writings.* Ed. Francois Matheron. London: Verso, 2003.

Arendt, Hannah. *Between Past and Future: Eight Exercises in Political Thought.* New York: Penguin Books, 1968.

Arendt, Hannah. *The Human Condition.* Chicago: University of Chicago Press, 1998.

Aristotle, *The Complete Works of Aristotle.* Trans. J. Barnes. Princeton: Princeton University Press, 1984.

Backer, David I. "Interpellation, Counterinterpellation, and Education." *Critical Education* 9, no. 15 (2018): 1-21.

Becker, Brian. "Raising Consciousness in the Anti-War Movement." *Liberation School,* 01 May 2006. Available here: https://www.liberationschool.org/06-05-01-raising-consciousness-in-antiwar-html.

Benjamin, Walter. *Gesammelte Briefe, Volume 1.* Ed. C. Gödde and H. Lonitz. Frankfurt am Main: Suhrkamp, 1995.

Benjamin, Walter. *Selected Writings, Volume 1, 1913-1926.*

Ed.. Bullock and M. W. Jennings. Cambridge, MA: Belknap Press, 2004.

Benjamin, Walter. *Selected Writings, Volume 2, Part 1, 1927-1930*. Ed. M.W. Jennings, H. Eiland, G. Smith. Cambridge, MA: The Belknap Press of Harvard University Press, 2005.

Benjamin, Walter. *Selected Writings: Volume 2, Part 2, 1931-1934*. Ed.. M. W. Jennings, H. Eiland, and G. Smith. Cambridge, MA: Belknap Press, 2005.

Benjamin, Walter. *Selected Writings, Volume 3, 1935-1938*. Ed. H. Eiland and M. W. Jennings. Cambridge, MA: Harvard University Press, 2002.

Benjamin, Walter *Selected Writings: Volume 4, 1938-1940*. Eds. H. Eiland and M. W. Jennings. Cambridge, MA: Belknap Press, 2003.

Benjamin, Walter. *The Arcades Project*. Ed. H. Eiland and K. McLaughlin. Cambridge, MA: Harvard University Press, 1999.

Biesta, Gert J.J. *Beyond Learning: Democratic Education for a Human Future*. Boulder: Paradigm Publishers, 2006.

Biesta, Gert J.J. *The Beautiful Risk of Education*. Boulder: Paradigm Publishers, 2014.

Charles, Matthew. "Secret Signals from Another World: Walter Benjamin's Theory of Innervation." *New German Critique* 45, no. 3 (2018): 39-72.

Debord, Guy. "Theory of the Dérive,. Trans. K. Knabb. In *Situationist International Anthology*. Ed. K. Knabb. Berkeley: Bureau of Public Secrets, 1958/1989.

Duttlinger, Carolin. "Between Contemplation and Distraction: Configurations of Attention in Walter Benjamin."

German Studies Review 30, no. 1 (2007): 33-54.

Esposito, Roberto. *Third Person.* Trans. Z. Hanafi. Cambridge: Polity Press, 2012.

Flusser, Vilém. *Gestures.* Trans. N.A. Roth. Minneapolis: University of Minnesota Press, 2014.

Ford, Derek R. *Communist Study: Education for the Commons*, 2nd. ed. Lanham: Lexington Books, 2022.

Ford, Derek R. *Encountering Education: Elements for a Marxist Pedagogy.* Madison: Iskra Books, 2022.

Freire, Paulo. *Pedagogy of the Heart.* Trans. D. Macedo and A. Oliveira. London: Continuum, 1997.

Freire, Paulo. *Pedagogy of the Oppressed.* Trans. M.B. Ramos. New York: Continuum, 2001.

Freire, Paulo. *The Politics of Education.* Trans. D. Macedo. Massachusetts: Bergin & Garvey Publishers, 1985.

Friedlander, Eli. *Walter Benjamin: A Philosophical Portrait.* Cambridge, MA: Harvard University Press, 2012.

Harney, Stefano and Fred Moten. *The Undercommons: Fugitive Planning & Black Study* (New York: Minor Compositions, 2013.

Hardt, Michael and Antonio Negri. *Assembly.* Cambridge, MA: Harvard University Press, 2017.

Hardt, Michael and Antonio Negri. *Commonwealth.* Cambridge, MA: Harvard University Press, 2009.

Hardt, Michael and Antonio Negri. *Declaration.* New York, NY: Argo Navis, 2012.

Hardt, Michael and Antonio Negri. *Empire.* Cambridge, MA: Harvard University Press, 2000.

Hardt, Michael and Antonio Negri. *Multitude: War and Democracy in the Age of Empire.* London: Penguin, 2005.

Higgins, Chris. "Human Conditions for Teaching: The Place of Pedagogy in Arendt's *Vita Activa*." *Teachers College Record* 112, no. 2 (2010): 407-445.

Higgins, Chris. *The Good Life of Teaching: An Ethics of Professional Practice.* London: Wiley-Blackwell, 2011.

Horkheimer, Marx and Theodor W. Adorno. *Dialectic of Enlightenment: Philosophical Fragments.* Trans. E. Jephcott. Stanford: Stanford University Press, 2007.

Jaeger, Werne. *Paideia: The Ideals of Greek Culture.* Trans. G. Highet. New York: Oxford University Press, 1944.

Jameson, Fredric. *Late Marxism.* London: Verso, 2000.

Kafka, Franz. *The Trial.* Trans. Breon Mitchell. New York: Schocken Books, 1998.

Krementz, Jill. *The Writer's Desk.* New York: Random House, 1996.

Lewis, Tyson E. "Capitalists and Conquerors Teaching Against Global Capitalism and the New Imperialism Rage and Hope: Interviews with Peter McLaren on War, Imperialism, and Critical Pedagogy." *Historical Materialism* 17, no. 1 (2009): 201-208.

Lewis, Tyson E. "Cities Gone Wild." *Postdigital Science and Education* 2 (2020): 597-600.

Lewis, Tyson E "Education and the Immunization Paradigm." *Studies in Philosophy and Education* 28, no. 6 (2009): 485-498.

Lewis, Tyson E. "Education for Potentiality (Against Instrumentality)." *Policy Futures in Education* 18, no. 7 (2020): 878-891.

Lewis, Tyson E. "Exopedagogy: On Pirates, Shorelines, and the Educational Commonwealth." *Educational Philosophy and Theory* 44, no. 8 (2012): 845-86.

Lewis, Tyson E. *Inoperative Learning: A Radical Rewriting of Educational Potentialities.* New York: Routledge, 2017.

Lewis, Tyson E. "Messianic Pedagogy." *Educational Theory* 60, no. 2 (2010): 231-248.

Lewis, Tyson E. "Move Around! There is Something to See Here: The Biopolitics of the Perceptual Pedagogy of the Arts." *Studies in Art Education* 57, no. 1 (2015): 53-62.

Lewis, Tyson E. "Study: A Disinterested Passion." In *Keywords in Radical Philosophy and Education: Common Concepts for Contemporary Movements.* Ed. D. Ford. Leiden: Brill, 2019.

Lewis, Tyson E. "Swarm Intelligence: Rethinking the Multitude from within the Transversal Commons." *Culture, Theory, and Critique* 51, no. 3: 223-238.

Lewis, Tyson E. *The Aesthetics of Education: Theatre, Curiosity, and Politics in the Work of Jacques Rancière and Paulo Freire.* London: Continuum, 2012.

Lewis, Tyson E. "The Dude Abides, or Why Curiosity is Important for Education Today." In *Curiosity Studies: A New Ecology of Knowledge.* Ed. P. Zurn and A. Shankar. Minneapolis: University of Minnesota Press, 2020.

Lewis, Tyson E. "Toward a Communist Philosophy of Education: Reflections on Method and Methodology." In *Communist Study: Education for the Commons.* By D.R. Ford. Lanham: Lexington Books, 2016.

Lewis, Tyson E. *Walter Benjamin's Anti-Fascist Education: From Riddles to Radio.* New York: SUNY Press, 2020.

Lewis, Tyson E. and Peter Hyland. *Studious Drift: Movements and Protocols for a Postdigital Education.* Minneapolis: University of Minnesota Press, 2022.

Lewis, Tyson E. and Daniel Cho. "Home is Where the Neurosis Is: A Topography of the Spatial Unconscious." *Cultural Critique* 64, Fall (2005): 69-91.

Lewis, Tyson E. amd Florelle D'Hoest. "Exhausting the Fatigue University: In Search of a Biopolitics of Research." *Ethics & Education* 10, no. 1 (2015): 49-60.

Lewis, Tyson E. and Steve Valk. "Educational Realism: Defining Exopedagogy as the Choreography of Swarm Intelligence." *Educational Philosophy and Theory* 54, no. 7 (2022): 906-915.

Lukács, Georg. *History and Class Consciousness: Studies in Marxist Dialectics*. Cambridge: MIT Press, 1971.

Marx, Karl. *Capital: Volume One*. London: Penguin Classics, 1990.

Lukács, Georg. *Lenin: A Study on the Unity of His Thought*. Cambridge, Mass.: MIT Press, 1971.

Masschelein, Jan and Maarten Simons. "Schools as Architectures for Newcomers and Strangers: The Perfect School as Public School?" *Teachers College Press* 112, no. 2 (2010): 531-555.

Masschelein, Jan and Maarten Simons. *In Defense of the School: A Public Issue*. Leuven, Belgium: E-Ducation, Culture, & Society, 2013.

Masschelein, Jan Maaren Simons, Ulrich Bröckling, and Ludwig Pongratz. *The Learning Society From the Perspective of Governmentality*. London: Wiley-Blackwell, 2007.

McLaren, Peter. *Capitalists and Conquerors: A Critical Pedagogy Against Empire*. Lanham: Rowman and Littlefield, 2005.

McLaren, Peter. *Che Guevara, Paulo Freire, and the Pedagogy of Revolution.* Lanham: Rowman & Littlefield, 2000.

Mitchell, Don. "A Complicated Fetish." *Social & Cultural Geography* 15, no. 2 (2014): 125-126.

Morrow, Raymond and Carlos Alberto Torres. *Reading Freire and Habermas.* New York: Teachers College Press, 2002.

Negri, Antonio. *The Savage Anomaly.* Trans. M. Hardt. Minneapolis: University of Minnesota Press, 1991.

Noddings, Nel. *Caring: A Relational Approach to Ethics and Moral Education.* Berkeley: University of California Press, 2013.

North, Paul. *The Problem of Distraction.* Stanford: Stanford University Press, 2011.

Plato. *Five Dialogues: Euthyphro, Apology, Crito, Meno, Phaedo.* Trans. G.M.A. Grube. Indianapolis: Hackett Publishing Company, 2002.

Plato. *Republic.* Trans. G. M. A. Grube. Indianapolis: Hackett Publishing Company, Inc., 1992.

Rancière, Jacques. *Althusser's Lesson.* Trans. E. Battista. New York: Continuum, 2011.

Rancière, Jacques. *The Aesthetic Unconscious.* Trans. D. Keates and J. Swenson. Cambridge: Polity Press, 2009.

Rancière, Jacques. *The Emancipated Spectator.* Trans. G. Elliott. London: Verso, 2009.

Rancière, Jacques. *The Ignorant Schoolmaster: Five Lessons in Intellectual Emancipation.* Trans. K. Ross. Stanford: Stanford University Press, 1991.

Rancière, Jacques. *The Philosopher and His Poor.* Trans. A. Parker. Durham: Duke University Press, 2004.

Rancière, Jacques. *The Politics of Aesthetics.* Trans. G. Rockhill. London: Continuum, 2004.

Rousseau, Jean-Jacques. *Emile: Or On Education.* Trans. A. Bloom. New York: Basic Books, 1979.

Sawyer, Caroline. "The Child Is Not a Person: Family Law and Other Legal Cultures." *Journal of Social Welfare and Family Law* 28, no. 1: 1-14.

Shutz, Aaron. "Is Political Education an Oxymoron? Hannah Arendt's Resistance to Public Spaces in Schools." In *Philosophy of Education Yearbook, 2001.* Urbana-Champaign: University of Illinois Press, 2001.

Taylor, Paul. *The Texts of Paulo Freire.* Buckingham: Open University Press, 1993.

Springgay, Stephanie. *Body Knowledge and Curriculum.* New York: Peter Lang, 2008.

Toppo, Gregg. "Good Grades Pay Off Literally." *USA Today,* 27 January 2008. Available here: http://www.usatoday.com/news/education/2008-01-27-grades_N.htm.

Young, Norman H. "Paidagogos: The Social Setting of a Pauline Metaphor." *Novum Testamentum* 29, no. 2 (1987): 150-176.

Zembylas. Michalinos. "Witnessing in the Classroom: The Ethics and Politics of Affect." *Educational Theory* 56, no. 3 (2006): 305–324.

Printed in the USA
CPSIA information can be obtained
at www.ICGtesting.com
CBHW021126050124
3203CB00005B/314